✦ GEM TRAILS OF ARIZONA ✦

by James R. Mitchell

Yavapai COLLEGE
ELDERHOSTEL

ARIZONA GEMS & MINERALS, INC
6370 E. HWY. 69
PRESCOTT VALLEY, AZ 86314
PH. (602) 772-6443

Gem Guides Book Co.
315 Cloverleaf Drive, Suite F
Baldwin Park, CA 91706

Library of Congress Catalog Number 94-74211
ISBN 0-935182-82-9

Introduction: Jeffrey Scovil and James R. Mitchell
Maps: Jean Hammond and John Mayerski
Cover: Marios Savvides

NOTE
    Due to the possibility of personal error, typographical error, misinterpretation of information, and the many changes due to man or nature, *Gem Trails of Arizona*, its publisher and all other persons directly or indirectly associated with this publication assume no responsibility for accidents, injury or any losses by individuals or goups using this publication.
    In rough terrain and hazardous areas all persons are advised to be aware of possible changes due to man or nature that can occur along the gem trails.

TABLE OF CONTENTS

SECTION I:

SECTION II:

SECTION III:

SECTION IV:

LOCATOR MAP

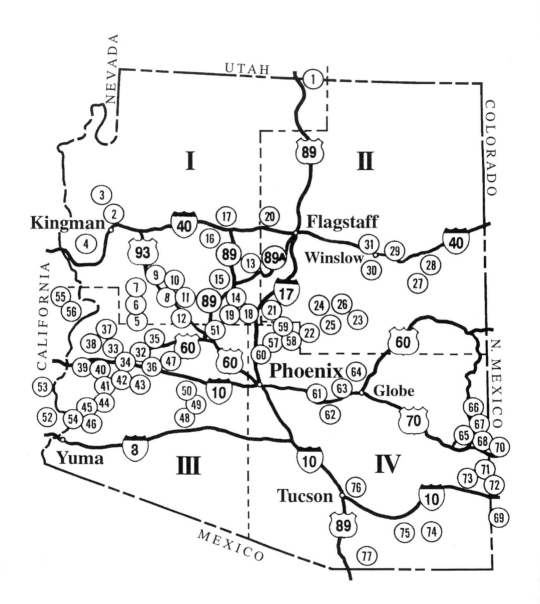

MAP LEGEND

▬▬▬	Interstate Highway
▬▬	U.S. Highway
▬▬	State Highway
▬▬	Divided Highway
———	Local Road
▬ ▪ ▪ ▪ ▬	Gravel Graded Road
▬▬	Graded Dirt Road
= = = = = = =	Unimproved Dirt Road
– – – – – – –	Trail
(10)	Interstate Highway
(60)	U.S. Highway
(71)	State Highway
[64]	Forest or County Road
⚒	Mine
≡	Cattle Guard
⊠	Gate
⬭	Pit
Λ	Campground

Each of the locations listed in the revised *Gem Trails of Arizona* was checked shortly before publication to verify mineral availability and to confirm that collecting was still allowed. In this edition, twenty-three new sites have been added, and a few of the less productive ones from the past edition have been eliminated. Keep in mind that some of the spots described are privately owned and a fee may be charged to collect there. That information is presented in the text.

Arizona is noted for its abundance of minerals and gemstones. Rockhounds come from all over the world to explore this scenic state, searching for its mineral treasures. Arizona is one of the most highly mineralized states in the country. Eight hundred and ten different mineral species have been identified here so far, 76 of them new to science.

The mines, hills and deserts of Arizona produce an incredible profusion of superb crystals and gem materials, some unique to the state and others the best in the world. For those with an interest in the lapidary arts, Arizona has a great deal to work with. Its gem production is among the highest in the United States.

The state is blessed with numerous deposits of agate, jasper, chalcedony, chert, petrified wood, peridot and turquoise among others. Wulfenite is much sought after by collectors, with Arizona boasting eight major and numerous minor localities for the beautiful mineral. The Red Cloud Mine north of Yuma is considered to be the premier locality in the world for bright orange-red crystals of wulfenite.

Arizona has also produced some of the world's best malachite and azurite. These green and blue carbonates of copper make both beautiful specimens and fine cutting material. Most of the world's cutting quality peridot comes from the San Carlos Indian Reservation here in Arizona.

The abundance of raw materials, great climate and beautiful scenery have made the state a Mecca for mineral and gem enthusiasts. It is no wonder that Arizona hosts two of the most famous mineral gatherings in the world each winter—The Tucson Gem and Mineral Show and the Quartzsite shows.

MINERAL HIGHLIGHTS

Petrified Wood

The petrified wood of Arizona is world renowned for its beauty and abundance. Arizona has been particularly blessed with localities for fine petrified wood, the most famous of which is the Petrified Forest near Holbrook. The forest is a national park and its 94,189 acres are part of the Painted Desert. As a national park, there is no collecting allowed, but there are numerous shops in the area that will sell you fine petrified wood. The deposits containing the wood extend for many miles beyond the forest boundaries, and there are a number of places where digging for wood is allowed on a fee basis.

One hundred and eighty to two hundred million years ago in what we call the upper Triassic Period, the area was part of a vast flood plain with many streams, small lakes and swamps. The area had a lush growth of ferns, horsetails, club mosses and trees. Animal life was also abundant with many amphibians, lungfishes and primitive dinosaurs. Most of the trees were Araucarioxylon arizonicum — similar to our modern Norfolk Pine. These ancient trees grew to heights of over 200 feet.

When the trees died, some fell and were buried near where they grew. Many others were washed downstream and were buried in giant log jams under many feet of sand and mud. These sediments eventually turned into the sandstones and shales of the Chinle formation. After burial, silica laden water seeping through the sediments slowly replaced the wood in the trees cell by cell, petrifying them. The silica was deposited as colorful agate, chalcedony and jasper. Hollows in the trees were sometimes lined with smoky quartz and amethyst crystals.

In the millions of years that followed burial and petrification, the region was uplifted and erosion eventually exposed many of the trees. The first record of the area was in the journal of Lorenzo Sitgreaves in 1851 who found the area barren and inhospitable. In the 1890s, wagon loads of logs were removed, and many of them dynamited for the amethyst and quartz crystals. In 1906 Teddy Roosevelt proclaimed the area a national monument, and the site became a national park in 1962. There are few places in the world that rival the colors, patterns and quantity of petrified woods found in Arizona.

Collectors are reminded of government regulations about gathering petrified wood. Rockhounds can obtain no more than 25 pounds of wood per day, plus one piece, and no more than 250 pounds per year. To acquire a specimen weighing more than 250 pounds, a permit must be procured from the district manager of the Bureau of Land Management. Groups cannot pool their allocations together. Wood from public lands can't be bartered or sold to commercial dealers and may be obtained only with hand tools.

Turquoise

One of Arizona's best known gem minerals is turquoise which is a hydrated copper aluminum phosphate. It is usually found in massive form, with a hardness of 5 to 6 on Moh's scale, which is relatively soft for a gemstone. It ranges from very soft and chalky to quite dense and solid. The color ranges from blue to blue-green to apple green.

Turquoise is formed by the action of surface water on aluminum-bearing rocks in the presence of copper in arid areas, which means it is frequently found in or near copper mines in the dry Southwest.

The three best known producing areas are the Mineral Park region near Kingman in Mohave County, Morenci in Greenlee County and Bisbee in Cochise County. The mines in the Mineral Park region that have produced quantities of fine turquoise are located on Ithaca Peak and Turquoise Mountain (formerly known as Aztec Mountain). Turquoise from the area typically has a spider web pattern of chalcopyrite in it. The area has been producing since 1883.

Material from the Morenci region is characterized by pyrite inclusions. Bisbee has produced primarily high quality, dense turquoise needing no stabilization. It often occurs as veins in massive pyrite from the Cole Shaft and the Lavender Pit.

Another well known producer is the Courtland-Gleeson area, in Cochise County. Gila County is blessed with several good turquoise localities: Canyon Creek, Castle Dome and Pinto Valley (which at one point was producing 9,000 pounds a month) and the Sleeping Beauty Mine of the Copper Cities area.

Chrysocolla

A mineral sometimes confused with turquoise is chrysocolla. While they both occur in shades of blue and are found in copper mining regions of the Southwest, they are quite different. Chrysocolla is a hydrated silicate of copper and aluminum. When pure, it is quite soft - less than 2.5 on Moh's scale. It is also very brittle, making it unsuitable for use in jewelry. One of the identifying characteristics of chrysocolla is that your tongue will stick to it because of its highly porous nature. Fortunately, this beautiful blue mineral often comes mixed with chalcedony, giving it the durability needed of a good gemstone. The finest material is of an even light blue color and is called "gem silica".

The best chrysocolla in Arizona comes from the Miami, Inspiration and Old Dominion mines near Globe. Large masses were found at these mines, often mixed with malachite making for very colorful cutting material. Sometimes these masses were coated with sparkling white quartz crystals making truly spectacular specimens.

The open pit mine in Bagdad has also produced some good quality chrysocolla, but not near the same quantity or quality as the Globe region. At the big San Manuel pit in Pinal County, good chrysocolla has been found with black inclusions of the copper mineral tenorite, making for some very attractive cut stones. Bisbee, of course, cannot be left out of the chrysocolla picture, having produced a small amount of fine material sometimes associated with azurite from the Cole Shaft.

Chrysocolla sometimes forms stunning pseudomorphs after other minerals. The original minerals have altered to chrysocolla without losing their original form. The Miami and Inspiration Mines as well as the open pit at Bagdad have all produced chrysocolla pseudomorphs after azurite that are up to two inches in length. In the mid 1970s, several pockets were found at the Ray Mine, in Ray, that produced bright blue pseudomorphs after azurite that are up to three inches long. At the Grand Reef Mine in Graham County, chrysocolla has replaced twinned crystals of cerussite.

Peridot

Peridot is the name given to the gem variety of the mineral olivene. Olivene is typically yellowish green and found in basic igneous rocks such as peridotites and basalts. It seldom forms good crystals, and is usually found as masses of grains. With a hardness of 6.5 on Moh's scale it is hard enough to wear with some care.

Most of the peridot used in the jewelry trade comes from one area in Arizona — Peridot Mesa on the San Carlos Apache Reservation in Gila County. The peridot occurs as large clusters of grains in basalt. The grains seldom reach more than a few carats in size. One record beater from this locality was over 20 carats.

The other well known locality in Arizona is Peridot Ridge in Buell Park, Apache County, about 10 miles north of Fort Defiance. The occurrence is very similar to Peridot Mesa, but has not been worked as extensively.

MINING IN ARIZONA

Arizona is known as the "Copper State", with good reason. Sixty-five percent of this country's copper production originates in Arizona, producing in 1993 alone, 2.54 billion pounds of the important metal. In 1992, Arizona also produced 60,089 troy ounces of gold, 5,015,702 ounces of silver and 30,770,172 pounds of molybdenum. Most of these metals were a by-product of copper mining.

Mining in Arizona goes back at least 10,000 years when the early Native Americans were big game hunters and quarried the chert and agate needed for their tools. As they became more settled, these early inhabitants also quarried a variety of minerals for use in pigments. These included azurite, malachite, gypsum and ochre. Salt was a valuable commodity and was gathered at several places in the state. It was also necessary to find good clay sources to create the pottery for which Arizona's Native Americans are so famed. A variety of minerals were used to create ornaments for personal adornment.

The best known of these is turquoise which was traded throughout the Southwest. Obsidian became an important material for the manufacture of tools, and it too was traded with those not fortunate enough to have a source nearby. A far less exciting, but none-the-less valuable material was the stone quarried for use in building the famous pueblo villages of northeast Arizona. Except for a few copper bells traded from Mexico, the Native Americans of pre-Colombian Arizona were unfamiliar with metals.

In the early 1500s, the Spaniards arrived with their thirst for gold and silver. Much prospecting and mining was done by the early Spaniards in the region. Their efforts were usually limited to small mines of rich deposits that they could work quickly with a few men, and then leave just as quickly before they were killed by the Indians.

By the early 1700s, the Jesuits had established a number of missions throughout southern Arizona, most founded by Father Eusebio Francisco Kino, after whom the mineral kinoite is named. There are numerous rumors that the Jesuits were involved in mining in many of the areas in which they had missions. There is no evidence to support this claim. The rumors, however, were the undoing of the Jesuits. The King of Spain felt that the Jesuits were mining silver and gold and not giving him his royal share. He eventually sent soldiers to remove the Jesuits from their missions in the New World. To this day there are many stories of lost Jesuit mines and caches of gold and silver.

In 1750, a group of Mexican miners discovered the rich copper deposits of Ajo. When they found what they thought was silver ore was actually copper ore, they abandoned their claims.

Most of the region became part of the United States in 1848 after the war with Mexico. The rest was obtained with the Gadsen Purchase in 1853. During the 1870s, most of the large copper deposits were found — Morenci and Globe in 1872, Bisbee in 1876, Jerome in 1877, Silverbell, Catalina Mountains and the Twin Buttes deposits about 1878. The rich silver deposits of Tombstone were found in 1879 and became the center of attention of the country for five years until the silver ran out. Copper deposits in the area later revived the rough western town so often portrayed in film and book. Many of Arizona's deposits were not seriously worked until completion of the railroads in the early 1880s.

Silver and gold were the main driving forces for the prospecting in Arizona, with the much more economically important copper deposits being found in the search for those more precious metals. A major blow was dealt to much of the western mining industry in 1893 when silver was dropped as the standard for U.S. currency. Silver prices dropped overnight and most silver mines shut down, many never to reopen. What saved many mining communities was

A portion of the Vulture Mine

copper. The age of electricity was just starting and demand for copper was increasing. Mining focused more and more on copper, causing new mines to open, and reopening many that had closed in 1886 when copper prices were at an all time low. Branch railroad lines were built to mining communities, prospecting increased and large amounts of capital were invested in the territory.

The mining industry grew through the turn of the century, with many of the small mines being consolidated by new, growing, large companies such as Phelps Dodge and the Copper Queen Consolidated Mining Company. In the late 1920s large copper deposits were opened in Canada and South America, flooding the market and dropping the price of copper. Shortly thereafter, large deposits were discovered in Africa, and then came the crash of 1929 dealing a death blow to the copper industry in Arizona.

Mining in Arizona slowly recovered, developing along new lines. Open pit mining that was born around the turn of the century became the norm as the rich, smaller vein deposits played out. During World War II, another setback occurred when all mines not considered vital to the war effort were closed down. Prospecting and small scale mining increased dramatically when controls on the price of gold were removed in the 1970s.

There is still a great deal of mineral wealth in Arizona's mountains and deserts. Some deposits have yet to be discovered, and others are just waiting for more favorable economic conditions. Estimated reserves in Arizona copper mines will allow us to operate at present levels for almost another 50 years.

MINERAL AND GEM COLLECTING IN ARIZONA

The sites described in this book are situated in landscapes as full of variety as the minerals themselves. The terrain varies from arid deserts to lofty pine covered peaks. Because of these immense differences, do some advance research on where you plan to visit. Don't take a trip to the desert during the sweltering summer months or to the high mountains during the winter. Doing so could not only result in an unpleasant trip but it could be dangerous. When venturing into some of the more remote areas it is a good idea to take extra drinking water, foul weather clothing and, possibly, some food, just in case you get delayed or stuck.

Most of the areas discussed on the following pages are fairly easy to get to, but road conditions can change. Severe weather can make good roads very rough and rough roads impassable, even with four-wheel drive. Do not attempt traveling where your vehicle was not designed to go.

Geography and Climate

Arizona can be divided roughly into three regions: The Plateau Region, the Mogollon Rim and the southern desert or basin and range province. The Plateau region makes up roughly the northern third of the state. Collecting is usually restricted to the warmer months due to inclement winter weather.

The land is made up of relatively flat lying sediments dissected by rivers producing spectacular canyon and mesa country with an average elevation of over 5,200 feet. Numerous plant fossils are found in this region, especially petrified wood. For the gem collector, this area holds most of the fine petrified wood in the state.

The region as a whole is poorly mineralized with little to interest the collector with the exception of some of the uranium/vanadium deposits. Most of the rocks of this region are sandstones with minor conglomerates, formed by the action of streams, lakes, rivers and wind. The sediments making up the rocks were cut and recut many times by streams and rivers, leaving many sand-filled channels. It is in these ancient, refilled channels that the uranium/vanadium deposits are found.

The primary uranium and vanadium minerals are uraninite and montroseite respectively. Just as with the copper deposits farther south, oxidation of these minerals produced a suite of diverse and sometimes colorful secondary minerals. Unfortunately, many of these minerals are not well crystallized, and are mostly in microscopic sizes.

Cutting the state roughly in two in a line running from northwest to southeast is the Mogollon Rim. This is a mountainous band with elevations in excess of 7,000 feet. The upper slopes of the mountains are heavily forested and the scenery quite beautiful. There are a fair number of mineral and gem deposits in the Rim country which is an ideal region to collect in especially during the summer months. Temperatures are relatively cool then, making it a welcome respite from the heat of southern Arizona. The area also has a number of fossil localities, mostly containing the shells of the creatures that teemed in the seas that once covered the area. Snowfall can be heavy in the winter, so collecting is usually restricted to the summer months.

The southern portion of the state is the classic desert that most people envision when they think of Arizona. The relatively level region is frequently broken by small chains of northwest/southeast trending mountains. The majority of Arizona's mineral wealth is concentrated in this region. The average elevation is around 1,700 feet and is very arid with an average rainfall of only seven inches. Temperatures in the summer frequently exceed 110°F, which means most collecting is done during the cooler months. In the winter when most collectors are active in southern Arizona, temperatures can range from the 70s during the day to close to freezing at night.

Collecting Sites

The supply of gems and mineral materials seems limitless and, best of all, many of the prime collecting sites are situated on public lands. DO NOT ASSUME, HOWEVER, THAT THIS GUIDE GIVES PERMISSION TO COLLECT! Land status changes frequently. If you have a suspicion that a particular site is no longer open, be sure to inquire before proceeding. If nothing can be determined locally, land ownership information should be available at the

County Recorder's office.

Be advised that some of the sites are located on the dumps of old abandoned mines. DO NOT, under any circumstances, enter shafts, and always be cautious when exploring the surrounding regions. There are often hidden tunnels, rotted ground and pits, as well as rusty nails, broken glass and discarded chemicals; all of which create a potential hazard.

Rockhound Rules

The following are a few basic rules that should always be followed no matter what state or country you are collecting in.

1) Tell someone where you are going and when you expect to return.
2) Do not collect alone — have at least one companion and preferably two.
3) Wear appropriate clothing — long pants, work boots, preferably with steel toes, a hard hat if working around vertical rock faces, heavy work gloves and protective eye wear if you are going to be hammering.
4) Research the area you are going to — what kind of vehicle is needed to get there, what is to be found, are there old mine shafts you should be aware of or other dangers, what kind of collecting equipment will you need and be sure to bring a map.
5) Always ask permission to enter property if possible.
6) Leave all gates in the position you found them.
7) Do not disturb livestock.
8) Never, ever litter. If possible, leave the place cleaner than it was when you arrived.
9) Do not "hog" the site or make it difficult for the next person to collect.
10) Do not leave pets or children unattended, they can get into serious trouble.
11) Never leave fires unattended, and do not light them in dry, hazardous conditions.
12) Bring a first aid kit with you.
13) Never enter abandoned mines without proper training, equipment and permission and never alone.

Although there are hundreds of places in Arizona to collect minerals, fossils and gem materials, there are places you cannot. You are never allowed to collect in national monuments or state parks. The collecting of vertebrate fossils or Indian artifacts is allowed only on private property, and then only with permission from the land owner. Most operating mines are off limits, with access rarely granted due to insurance restrictions and interruption of the production schedule.

Outdoor Arizona

When collecting you must also be aware of possible dangers from animals, insects and plants. Always look where you are stepping or putting your hands.

Be careful when turning over rocks, as they may cover a creature that is not happy about being uncovered. Dangers from Arizona plants and wild life can be anything from annoying to deadly.

Be careful of cacti, they have a way of sneaking up on you. Watch where you sit and what you brush against. Never eat any wild plants unless you are absolutely sure you know what you are doing, many plants are very toxic. It would be wise to familiarize yourself with Arizona's common and toxic plants.

Arizona also has a variety of poisonous insects and arachnids including bees, wasps, fire ants, assassin bugs, black widow spiders, brown recluse spiders and scorpions. Always check your boots and gloves before putting them on, as well as other items of clothing.

Our most dangerous animals belong to the reptile group, and snakes in particular. Arizona is the home for a number of different types of rattlesnakes who you cannot always count on to give you a warning by their rattling. It is a good idea to learn what to do in case of rattlesnake bite. The best way to deal with snakes is to be aware and avoid them. Never walk blindly into rocky areas where they love to hide. Always look where you are stepping and if you do see a rattlesnake — stay away from it. Unless it is an immediate threat, do not kill it. Snakes have a part in the great scheme of things and help keep the rodent population down.

Parts of southern Arizona are the home to one of the few venomous lizards in the world — the Gila Monster. They are relatively rare and not aggressive, and so are little danger. They do not strike like a snake, but must get a firm hold on you to slowly work their poison into the wound. They are a species that should also be admired and left alone. Again, familiarize yourself with the poisonous animals of Arizona in your local library or book store.

MORE THAN JUST PRETTY ROCKS

Arizona is a state where there is plenty to see and do, beyond searching for minerals. When many people think of Arizona, visions of desolate and barren deserts usually come to mind. Granted, the state does boast some stark areas, but it is also a vacationer's paradise. There is spectacular Lake Powell, the beautifully sculpted and colorful geological wonderlands of the north in Monument Valley, Canyon de Chelly, Navajo National Monument, the Painted Desert, and, of course, the Grand Canyon.

Tourists are also drawn to the magnificent mountains near Flagstaff, where skiing is a common winter recreation. The cool pines and refreshing streams and rivers within the central mountainous band, stretching from Prescott, in the west, to the New Mexico border, have drawn vacationers for decades.

Visitors also have many chances to visit the Indian Country, boasting current tribal life, situated amongst remnants of the distant past. There is Navajo National Monument, Walnut Canyon National Monument, Wupatki National Monument, Montezuma Castle National Monument, and hundreds of other less accessible reminders of those who lived in this region so many years ago. If you take some time to plan your collecting trip properly and make sure your vehicle is in good working order, the gem fields and other sights and attractions of Arizona will provide you and your family with outstanding minerals and many memorable experiences.

As with any state in the country, Arizona is home to many amateur mineral and gem clubs. They can be found in nearly any town of reasonable size. To locate them you can ask at local rock and lapidary shops listed in the yellow pages, through the local chamber of commerce or natural history museums. Schools and colleges may also be able to help you find local clubs. Many communities have museums of natural history, mining or history which may contain exhibits of interest to collectors. They also often have libraries full of useful information and may even have lists of local clubs, the dates of gem and mineral shows as well as field trip information.

Enjoy your collecting and the wonderful hobby that we all share. Be safe, obey the laws and be considerate and we will have a hobby for many years to come. Remember, all it takes is one thoughtless person to close down a rock collecting locality.

This is certainly one of the most unique collecting localities to be discussed in this book. There is no need for four-wheel drive vehicles; instead you must have access to a dependable boat. The shores of Lake Powell are extensive. One could spend months exploring the innumerable beaches and side canyons without coming close to seeing all of the lake.

Try to explore as much of the shore as possible. Rockhounds can find a plethora of collectibles, even though they are somewhat scattered. There is agate and jasper, in just about every color imaginable, as well as petrified wood, fossils, interestingly weathered sandstone, obsidian, and a host of other lesser minerals, some of which is of very high quality. In addition to the potential for good mineral collecting, Lake Powell is one of the most spectacular bodies of water in the entire country, situated within the magnificent sandstone cliffs of Glen Canyon.

Start in any of the marinas along the lake, and carefully examine the landscape as you pass by. Any time you spot lots of rocks, especially in conjunction with sandy beaches, you will be in a region offering high collecting potential. The sand is usually a result of erosion up in the hills where the often beautiful agate, jasper, petrified wood and other stones were formed.

When you spot a potentially interesting beach, carefully maneuver your boat to the shore, securely anchor, and commence your inspection. The beaches and side canyons near Hole-In-The-Rock seem to be particularly productive, so be sure to make that region part of your journey. Most of the Lake Powell material stands out vividly in contrast to the common rocks, and they are usually easy to spot against the light colored sand. Using a rake to sift through the soil can also prove to be helpful, especially when in an area containing lots of good quality surface minerals. If you don't find much at your first stop, boat a little further along until you spot another high potential place where you can safely stop, and try again.

This is definitely not a collecting location for rockhounds in a rush. It must be worked in as part of a relaxing vacation. If you allow sufficient time, however, this could well be one of the most memorable rockhounding trips you have ever taken.

Due to the extensive nature of this site, no map has been included.

This site features white and delicately banded onyx, most of which is solid and capable of taking a high polish. At time of publication, the deposit was protected by a claim held by the Mojave County Gem Stoners Club of Kingman. Amateur rockhounds are allowed to gather specimens at no charge. If, when you visit, it appears that the status may have changed, be sure to inquire locally before collecting.

To reach the site from Kingman, take Interstate 40 to Exit 51, the Stockton Hill Road turnoff, and go north ten and one-tenth miles, as shown on the map. As you approach the given mileage, diggings can be seen on the lower slopes of the hill to the left, which marks the center of the collecting area. There are some ruts, leading about 100 yards off the main road, to the small quarry. Vehicles with high-clearance should have little difficulty getting in. If you have any doubts about your automobile's ability to get to the dumps, park off the main road and hike the short distance.

The best onyx is generally found where it was formed in the hillside, and it takes lots of work to remove sizable specimens. Gads, chisels, gloves, goggles and heavy hammers are needed to properly work here, but the fine quality of the material usually makes the effort worth it. If you don't feel like engaging in such labor, don't eliminate this site. There is plenty of onyx lying throughout the rubble on and around the dumps, and lots can be gathered by simply examining those areas. Much of the loose material tends to be somewhat small and weathered. Be certain to carefully examine everything that looks promising before deciding whether or not it should be saved.

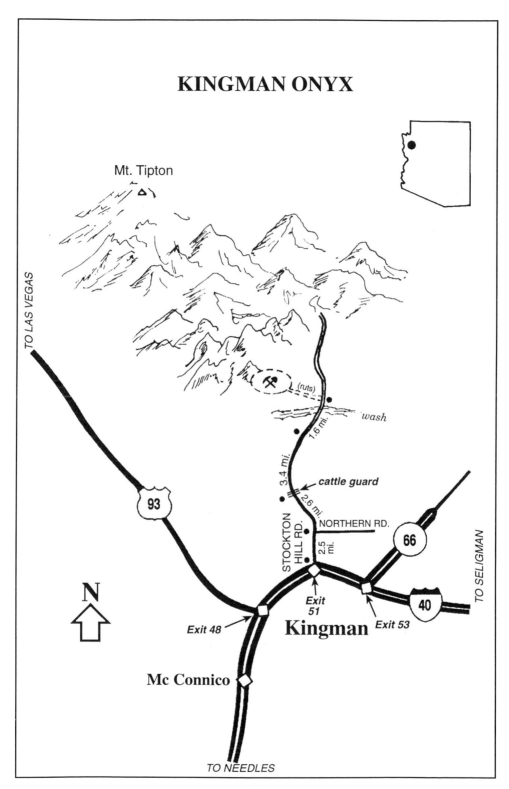

KINGMAN ONYX

Mt. Tipton

TO LAS VEGAS

(ruts)

wash

1.6 mi.

3.4 mi.

cattle guard

2.6 mi.

93

STOCKTON HILL RD.

NORTHERN RD.

66

2.5 mi.

TO SELIGMAN

N

Exit 51

40

Kingman

Exit 48

Exit 53

Mc Connico

TO NEEDLES

Only a short distance off busy Highway 93 is the once-bustling mining town of Chloride. Very little prospecting is currently being done in the hills surrounding what is left of the town. The dumps that remain offer a good variety of mineral specimens to collectors willing to spend some time and effort. The original silver/gold deposit was discovered in the mid-1800s, but it wasn't until the turn of the century that the town's population peaked at nearly 2,000 inhabitants. By 1950, however, most of the mining had ceased, leaving many of the mines abandoned. Today, there are still a few hardy prospectors working the region, but the number seems to get less and less each year.

Minerals of interest to collectors include bornite, chalcocite, vanadinite, galena, stibnite, chalcopyrite, iron pyrite, feldspar, black tourmaline, rose quartz, molybdenite, silver, and gold, including some spectacular wire gold. There are numerous lesser minerals available, but none in quantities large enough to be of interest.

The most prominent of the Chloride prospects is the Tennessee Mine, which is situated at the end of town, and can easily be seen as you approach. If driven carefully, that dump is accessible by a passenger car. Most of the other dumps in the vicinity can only be reached in high-clearance, four-wheel drive vehicles, or by hiking. As you search the dumps and areas of erosion below, most of the rock will appear somewhat the same. This is due to surface oxidation and weathering. It is usually necessary to split any suspect stones in order to expose fresh surfaces which can be more accurately examined for mineral content.

The turnoff to Chloride is well marked on Highway 93, and the road is paved until you reach town. Plan to spend a little time exploring the shops, and be sure to ascertain which dumps are abandoned and open to collecting, before picking up any specimens.

Old foundations on one of the Chloride dumps

CHLORIDE MINERALS

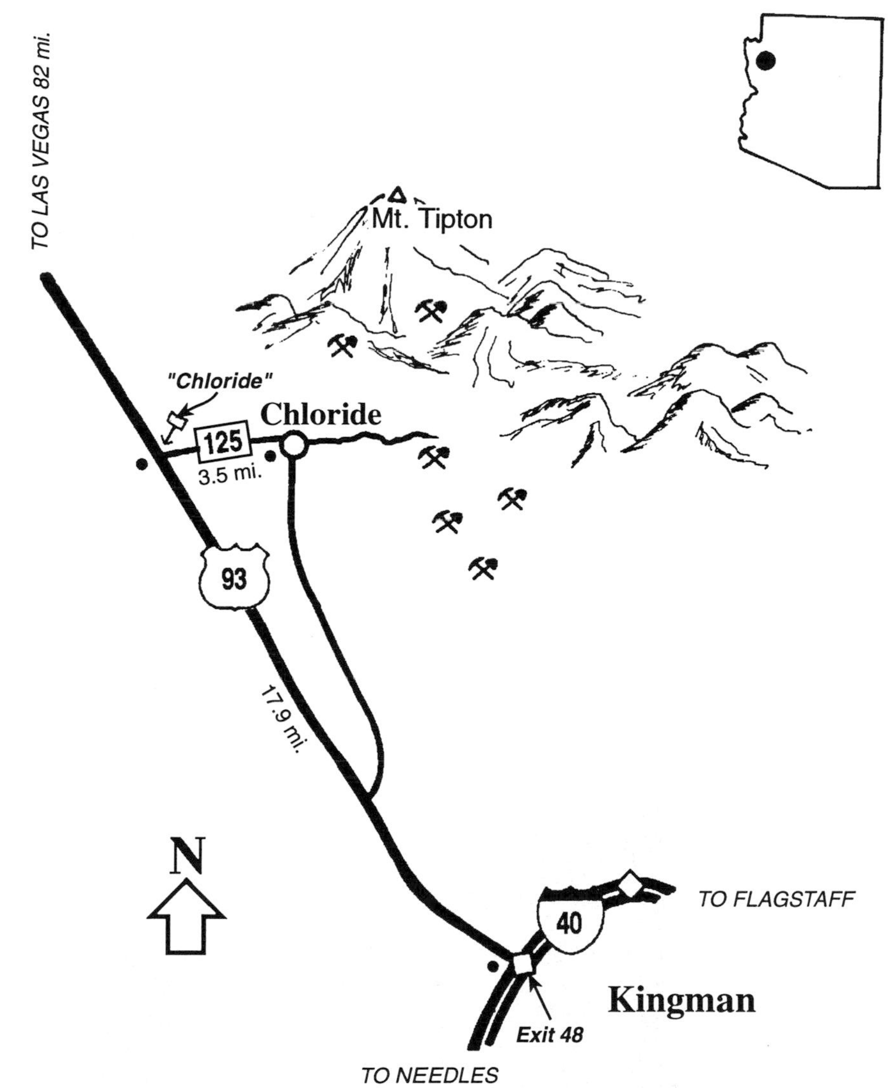

TO LAS VEGAS 82 mi.

Mt. Tipton

"Chloride"

Chloride

125

3.5 mi.

93

17.9 mi.

N

TO FLAGSTAFF

40

Kingman

Exit 48

TO NEEDLES

This is one of Arizona's best known fire agate locations. The claims have been open to collectors willing to pay a small fee for quite a few years. At time of publication, the charge is $5.00 per person, per day, with no limit on how much can be obtained. All colors of the rainbow can be found, including a rare black variety.

It is suggested that you bring a rock pick, shovel, small screw driver, whisk broom, sledge hammer, 3-4 foot pry bar, spray bottle with water, some small chisels, and a bucket or bag. Be advised that it is not an easy matter to locate the elusive fire agate. Lots of perseverance, skill and luck are required to find the best the site has to offer. To further increase the challenge, overburden is not removed by the owners and collectors are not permitted to use powered equipment or explosives.

Everyone is required to sign a waiver of liability in the event of injury while collecting. It is suggested that you check in at nearby Ed's Camp for current information. While you are there you will be able to see jewelry made from the fire agate and possibly get some collecting tips.

The site is easily reached from Kingman or Oatman, and the large sign denoting the Cuesta Fire Agate Mines can't be missed. The sign is situated just off old Highway 66, as it winds its way through the scenic Sacramento Mountains. The claims are usually open during the fall, winter, and spring. Dry camping is customarily allowed.

Be sure to drive by the ruins of Goldroad and allow some time to explore the shops in Oatman. This is a very scenic region, and the fire agate is only one of the many areas of potential interest to rockhounds.

Sign alongside highway designating collecting area

OATMAN FIRE AGATE

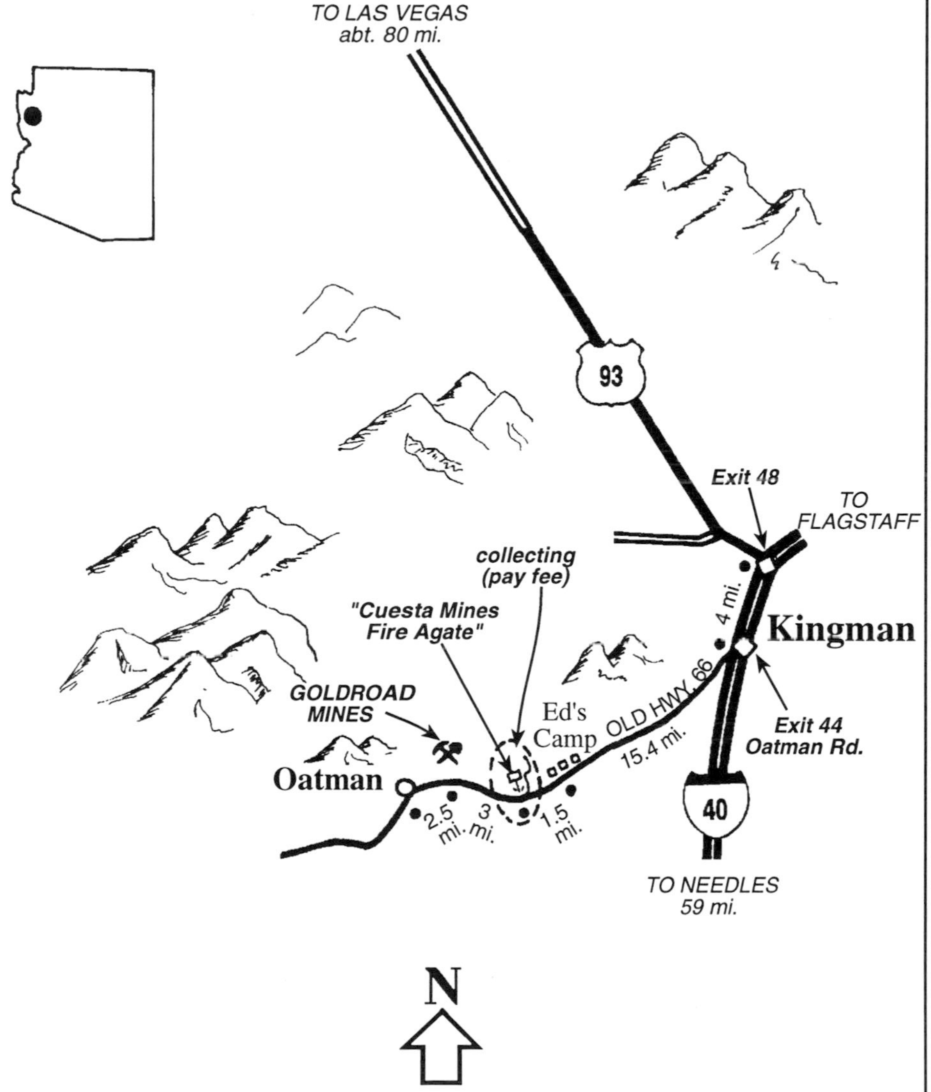

TO LAS VEGAS
abt. 80 mi.

93

Exit 48

TO
FLAGSTAFF

collecting
(pay fee)

"Cuesta Mines
Fire Agate"

Kingman

4 mi.

GOLDROAD
MINES

Ed's
Camp

OLD HWY 66

Exit 44
Oatman Rd.

Oatman

15.4 mi.

40

2.5
mi.

3
mi.

1.5
mi.

TO NEEDLES
59 mi.

N

This site features interesting manganese ores, as well as onyx, palm bog and agate. To get there from Wenden, go north on the Alamo Lake Road twelve and one-half miles to where the pavement veers to the right. Instead of following the main route, go directly ahead onto the dirt pipeline road. Proceed another twelve and nine-tenths miles, over the mountains, to where ruts can be seen leading east into a wash. Follow that wash about seven-tenths of a mile and then go onto the dim road leading to the old manganese mine, four-tenths of a mile further.

Be very careful around the mine, since the tunnels and shafts are rotten and could be very dangerous. In addition, there are a few mining claims nearby and you shouldn't collect within their boundaries.

Onyx can be found in the canyon about 100 yards north of the mine. It is fairly easy to spot, occurring in pastel hues of red and green. Some of the onyx is delicately banded, while others display solid colors and interesting patterns. The agate and palm bog litter the higher ground, and some of the palm is opalized, making it especially desirable. Most is found in the gray hills to the south and can be picked up from the surface or excavated from the soft soil by using a pick and shovel. The dendritic agate is frequently filled with interesting inclusions, and it takes an excellent polish.

This is a remote collecting area, so be certain your vehicle is in good repair and you have some extra supplies on hand in the event you are delayed.

Exploring the mining area at the collecting site

WENDEN DENDRITIC AGATE

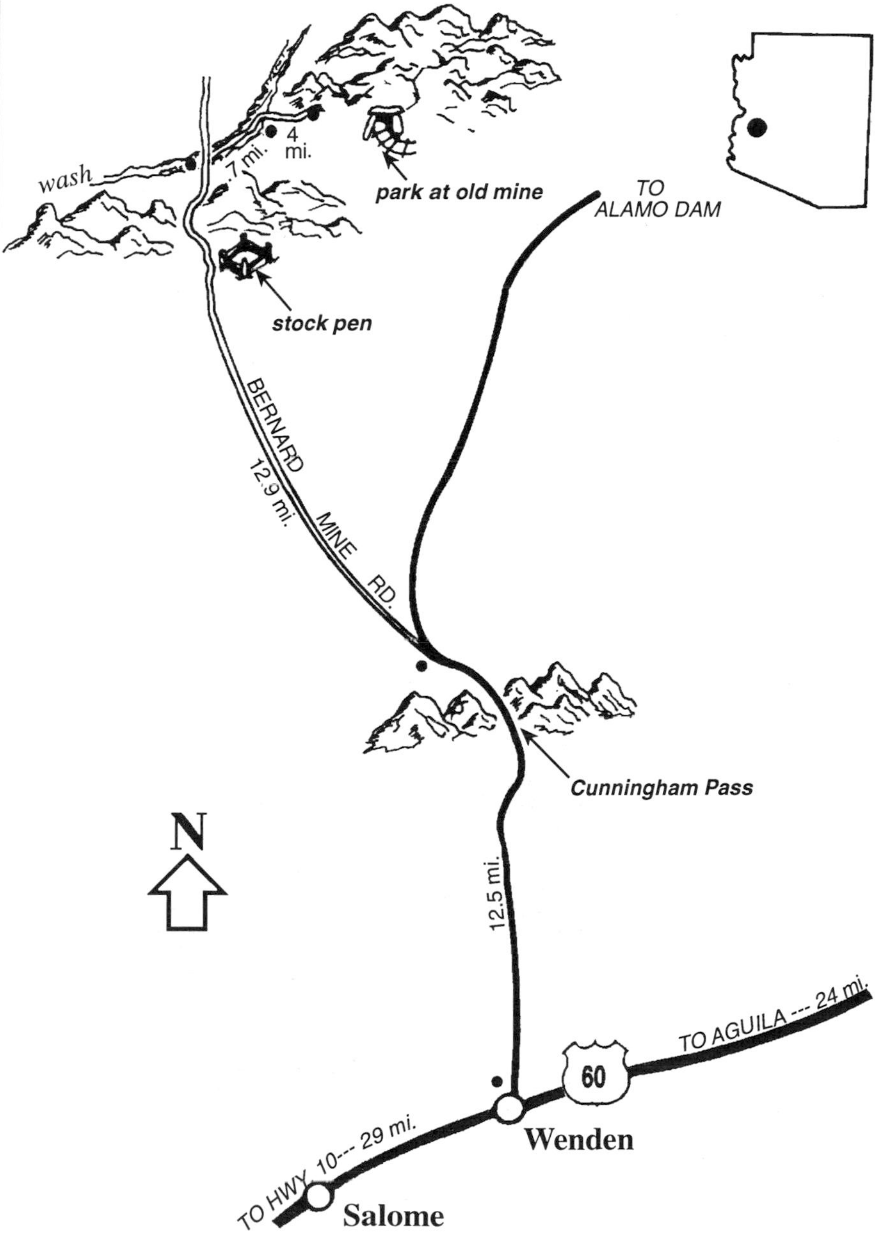

wash

.7 mi.

4 mi.

park at old mine

TO
ALAMO DAM

stock pen

BERNARD   MINE   RD.

12.9 mi.

Cunningham Pass

12.5 mi.

N

TO AGUILA --- 24 mi.

60

TO HWY 10--- 29 mi.

Wenden

Salome

Palm bog is a somewhat rare form of petrified palm wood. It was formed from the roots of palm trees growing in marshy areas and looks like petrified palm filled with large "eyes". When cut and polished, extremely interesting cabochons and other lapidary items can be made from this highly desirable material.

This site not only features outstanding samples of the palm bog, but, also petrified wood, agate, jasper and rhyolite. To get there, go north from Wenden on the Alamo Lake Road approximately twenty-seven and one-half miles. At that point, a dirt road heads off to the right toward the Wayside Inn, and you should follow it three and two-tenths miles. From there, turn left, go two and six-tenths miles, and, just after crossing the cattle guard, turn right. Continue another five and six-tenths miles and bear right again, just before reaching the lake. Drive one more mile and then take the right fork up the hill another two-tenths of a mile. At that point, the road crosses a light colored clay ridge which marks the primary collecting site.

Roam through the little canyon and search the terrain surrounding the ridge for agate, jasper, banded and swirled rhyolite and petrified wood. Nothing is particularly large, but most is suitable for producing nice size cabochons. The palm bog makes especially desirable stones, being filled with tiny lines, swirls, and "eyes" and it is generally a pleasing tan to brown in color.

This entire region, extending for many miles, is covered with collectibles, and randomly searching just about anywhere should be fruitful. Be certain, however, not to collect within the boundaries of Alamo Lake State Park, since rockhounding is not allowed in any Arizona state park. There are also lots of rattlesnakes in the area, so always be cautious.

Palm wood

ALAMO LAKE PALM BOG

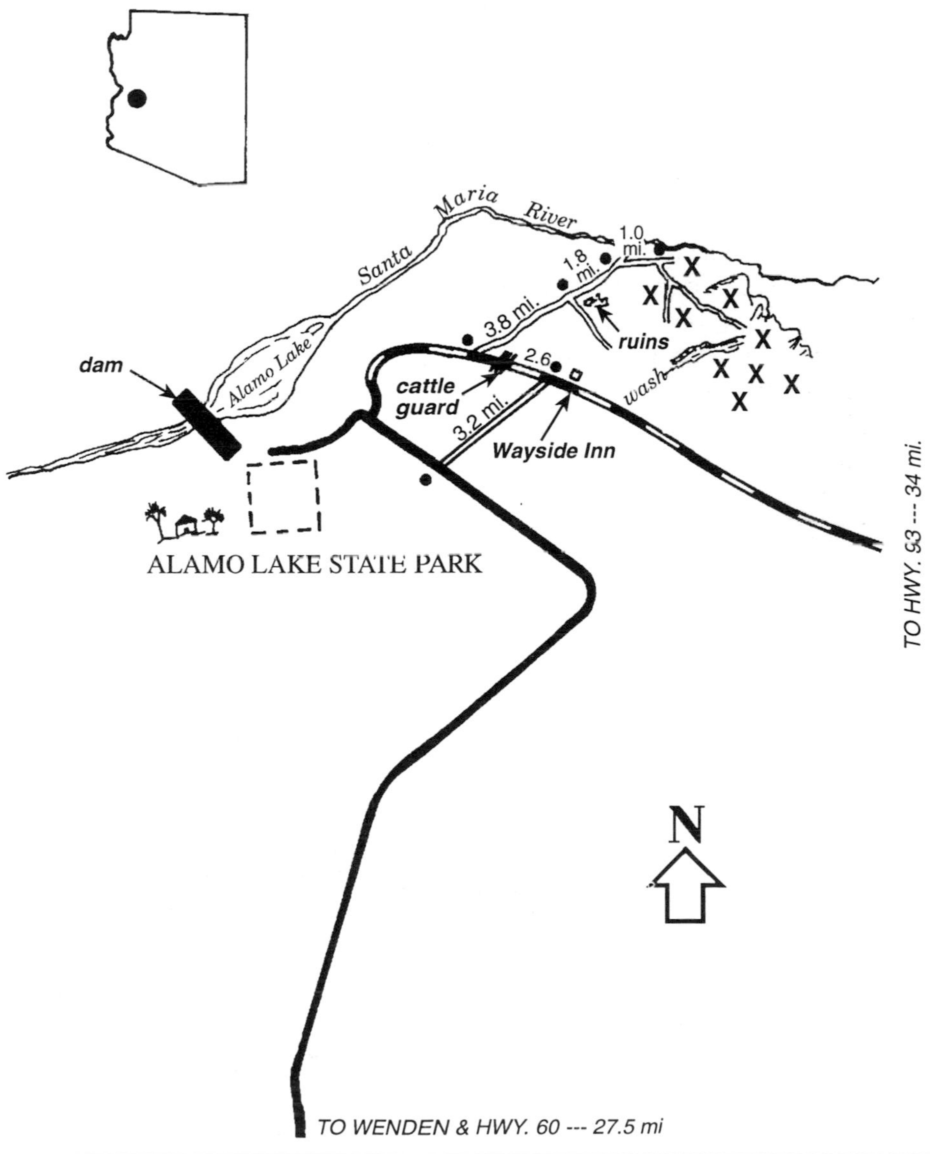

dam

Santa Maria River

Alamo Lake

1.0 mi.

1.8 mi.

3.8 mi.

ruins

2.6

cattle guard

3.2 mi.

Wayside Inn

wash

ALAMO LAKE STATE PARK

TO HWY. 93 --- 34 mi.

N

TO WENDEN & HWY. 60 --- 27.5 mi

Outstanding specimens of chert, agate, jasper, feldspar, mica, petrified wood and petrified palm can be found in the three extensive sites illustrated on the accompanying map. To get to Site "A", go west on Signal Road, which intersects Highway 93 eight and one-half miles south of Wikieup. The dirt road is well graded, and should not present a problem to any rugged vehicle. After having gone seventeen and one-half miles, turn left and proceed four and two-tenths miles to where a sandy wash intersects from the east. If you have four-wheel drive, follow that wash about seven-tenths of a mile, and, at that point, on the cliffs to the south, one can find pink feldspar, often associated with delicate books of mica, some of which can be trimmed into excellent display pieces.

Another one and six-tenths miles along the main road is Site "B". This location features a wide variety of collectibles, including colorful jasper, chert and petrified wood. Simply roam the slopes, on both sides of the road, keeping a keen eye to the ground. Specimens don't tend to be very large, but the quality more than makes up for that deficiency.

The most productive of all three sites is the vast region labeled Site "C", situated another ten and four-tenths miles farther south. Park anywhere within the area and look for agate, jasper, petrified wood, petrified palm, and petrified palm bog scattered randomly throughout the surrounding terrain. Some specimens are sizable, and most is of very good quality, capable of taking a high polish.

This is a very remote collecting location, and it is imperative that your vehicle is in good repair before visiting.

Collecting petrified wood

SIGNAL PETRIFIED WOOD

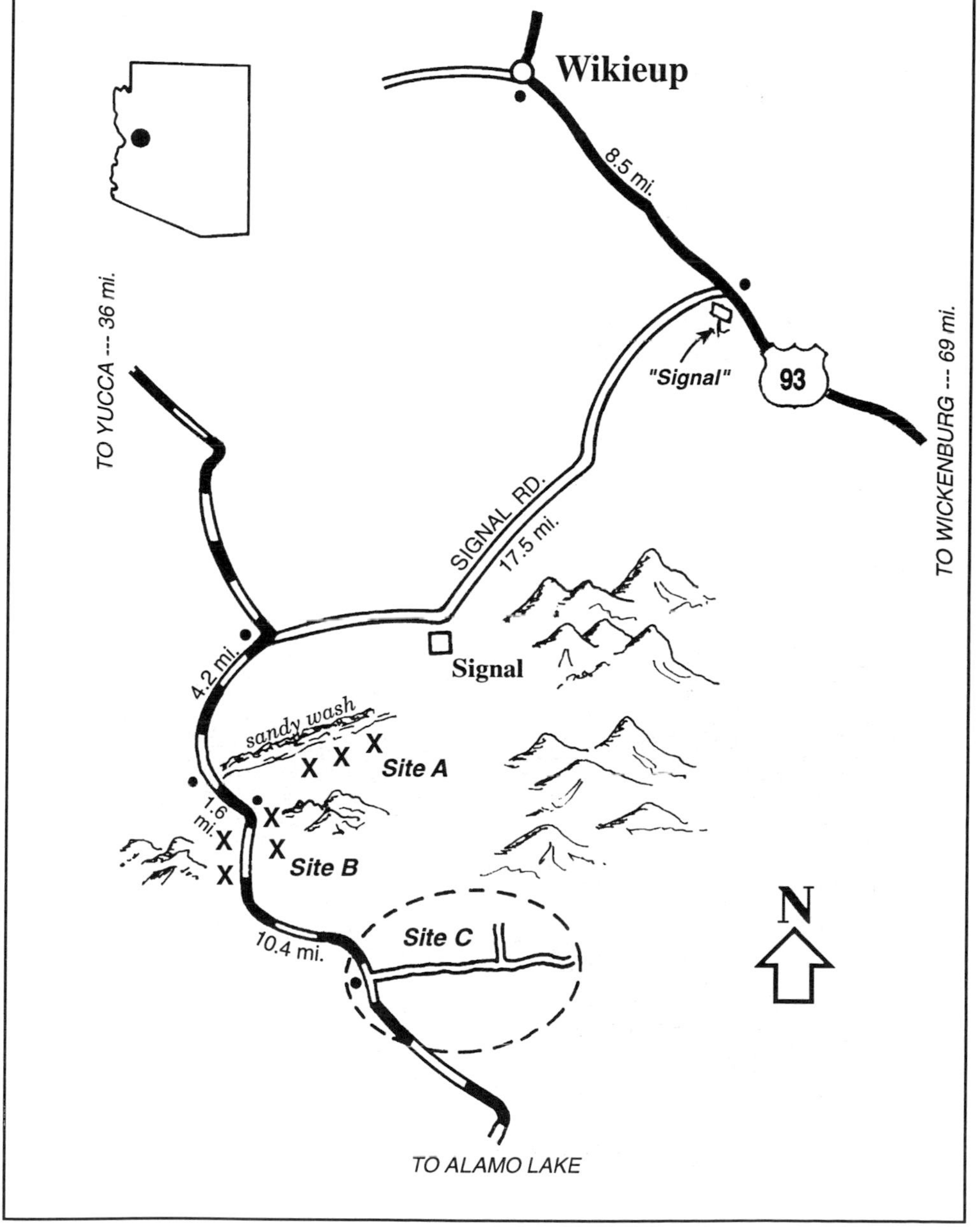

Wikieup

8.5 mi.

TO YUCCA --- 36 mi.

TO WICKENBURG --- 69 mi.

"Signal"

93

SIGNAL RD.

17.5 mi.

Signal

4.2 mi.

sandy wash

X X X Site A

X

X

X Site B

1.6 mi.

10.4 mi.

Site C

N

TO ALAMO LAKE

This site is easy to get to and most vehicles should be able to make the journey with no problem. To get there, go four and one-tenths mile north on Highway 93 from where it crosses over Highway 71. At that point, Alamo Road intersects from the left, and there is a stop sign, just off the pavement, to help identify the road. Proceed west on that well-graded dirt road five and eight-tenths miles to where ruts will be seen heading off to the north. Follow them about eight-tenths of a mile, turn right, go a short distance and park. The collecting extends for quite a distance in all directions. The roses are easy to spot due to their white color, which stands out vividly against the darker soil.

The area has long been known by collectors. Even though the site is extensive, much of the prime surface material seems to have been picked up over the years. It never fails, though, after every major rainstorm, a new crop of the delicate chalcedony roses seem to appear.

If you have time, the best way to find well-formed specimens, is to hike away from the roads. Pay particularly close attention to washes and other areas of erosion throughout the region shown on the map, including the foothills of nearby Fire Mountain and the surrounding flatlands.

Desert landscape at the collecting site

DESERT ROSES

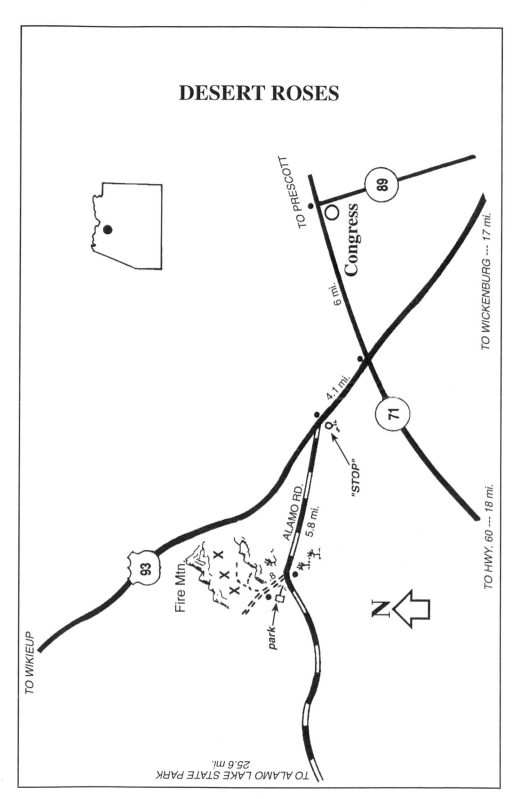

The region just east of the Highway 93 Burro Creek bridge is one of Arizona's premier rockhounding areas. To get to the center of this most productive locality, go seven miles on the graded dirt road leading off Highway 97, as shown on the map. Just before crossing the creek, a road intersects from the right, and it will take you to Sites "A" and "B".

Follow that road two and one-half miles and turn right onto the ruts another one-tenth of a mile. From that point and continuing a good distance, especially near the hills, one can find lots of top quality agate, opalite and pastelite. A few digging areas will be seen. If you feel up to tackling the seams with sledge, gads and chisels, the work could be well rewarded.

If you have four-wheel drive, proceed one and one-half miles farther along the main road to a wash. Follow the wash another two miles to where a white bank will be encountered. The white bank marks Site "B". Colorful opalized bentonite can be found about three to four feet deep in the white clay, sometimes being covered with light green opalite. This is a prime area of interest at Burro Creek, but be willing to do some tough digging to obtain worthwhile quantities.

Additional collecting can be accomplished by returning to the graded dirt road, crossing Burro Creek, and going another eight-tenths of a mile. At that point, pastelite, opalite and occasional chunks of jasper and agate will be found scattered all over. Take the tracks leading west toward the obvious white outcrop, about three-tenths of a mile past the creek. There, tons of white and gray pastelite can be procured, some being filled with interesting inclusions. This is labeled Site "C" on the map.

Continue north along the main road another seven-tenths of a mile to the power lines and explore the surrounding terrain. This locality boasts pink, orange, white and gray pastelite, opalite and agate. A gas line road is intersected four-tenths of a mile farther north and more material can be found at that intersection. The best is procured, however, by proceeding four-tenths of a mile west along the pipeline road, turning left and continuing another one-tenth of mile to Site "D". The ground is covered with colorful agate and jasper, as well as light green, orange, gray and white pastelite.

BURRO CREEK OPALITE

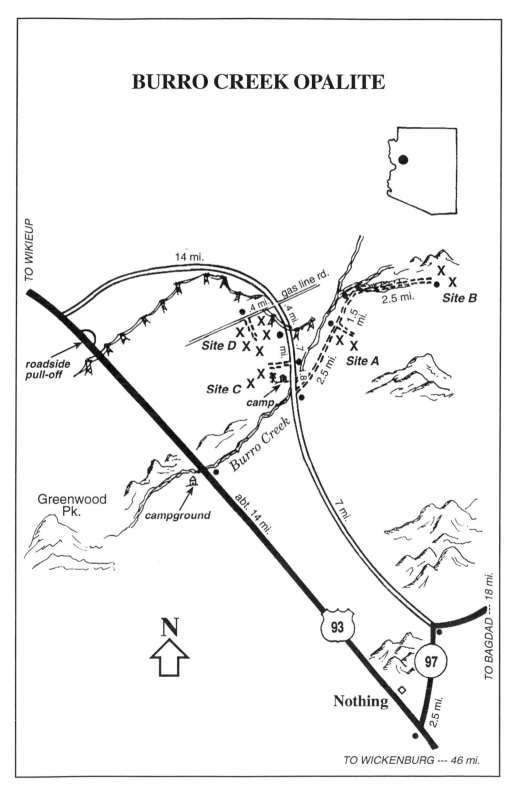

TO WIKIEUP

14 mi.

gas line rd.

roadside
pull-off

.4 mi.

.4 mi.

Site D X X X

Site C X X

camp

X X X

Site A

.7 mi.

1.8 mi.

2.5 mi.

1.5 mi.

2.5 mi.

X X

Site B

Burro Creek

Greenwood
Pk.

campground

abt. 14 mi.

7 mi.

N

93

97

Nothing

TO BAGDAD --- 18 mi.

2.5 mi.

TO WICKENBURG --- 46 mi.

The region surrounding Burro Creek is well known among rockhounds for the wide variety of cutting material that can be obtained there. To get to this renowned site from Highway 93, proceed to the tiny town of Nothing, Arizona, turn right onto Highway 97 and go two and one-half miles. At that point, proceed left onto the dirt road leading over the hill and down into the little canyon, approximately seven miles. At the given mileage, you should be at Burro Creek and the collecting is done throughout the hills and flatlands on both sides of the river, as shown on the map. The road to the creek is well graded and most rugged vehicles should not have difficulty making the trip.

The pastelite is not hard to find due to its colorful nature and plentiful supply. If willing to spend time exploring the area, you should be able to get a good quantity, some in delicate shades of pink, orange, brown and a variety of mixed colors. If not satisfied with what can be found scattered throughout the lowlands, you can attack any of the numerous seams in an effort to obtain additional specimens. This is tough work, but the rewards often make it worthwhile. You will need a sledge hammer, chisels, gads, pry bar, gloves and goggles if you do attack the seams.

If you plan to spend a few days here, there is a nice campground only a short distance away, as shown on the map.

Pastelite collecting area

BURRO CREEK PASTELITE

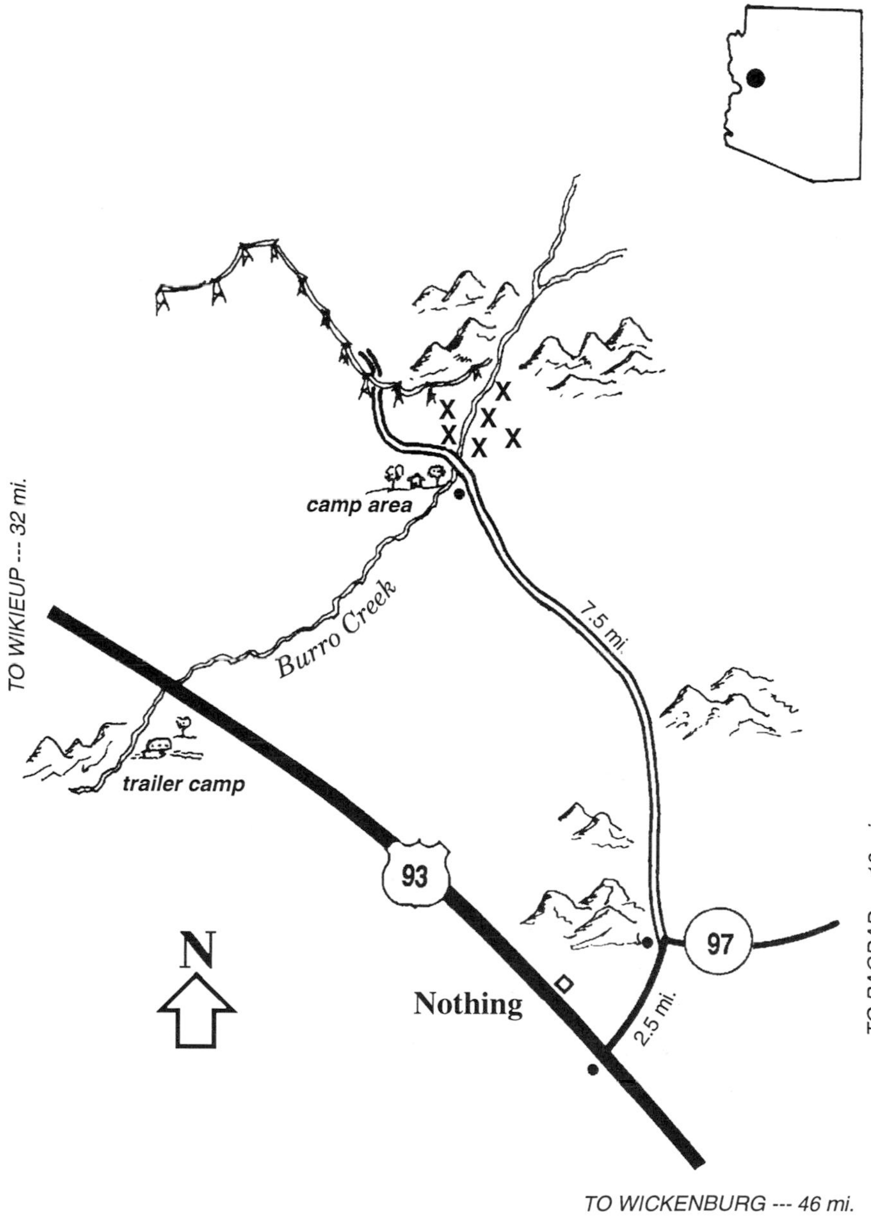

X X
X
X X X

camp area

Burro Creek

7.5 mi.

TO WIKIEUP --- 32 mi.

trailer camp

93

N

Nothing

97

2.5 mi.

TO BAGDAD --- 18 mi.

TO WICKENBURG --- 46 mi.

The Apache tears found at this site are a little different than those obtained at other locations. Here, the stones do not sparkle in the sunlight, looking something like small chunks of charcoal. For that reason, when collecting, you should walk away from the sun, not toward it, as is normal procedure. By searching in this manner, the tears will look like dark black pebbles in the lighter colored soil and thereby be fairly easy to spot.

Two types of Apache tears can be found. They appear identical on the surface, but tumbling to remove the crust will reveal that some are opaque and others are beautifully banded. The banded stones exhibit light and dark areas and a few will even produce a chatoyant or cat's-eye effect. The opaque variety may be substituted for jet black onyx, or cut thin and used for backing material in opal doublets.

To get to the center of the site, follow Highway 93 north about fifty-nine miles from Wickenburg to the large bridge spanning Burro Creek. The tears are scattered throughout the highlands overlooking the river for quite a distance. The greatest concentration seems to be on the flat mesa and its lower slopes, situated about one-half mile south of the bridge.

There is a nice BLM campground, as shown on the map, and it can serve as a pleasant base for Burro Creek rockhounding.

Apache tears found at the collecting area

BURRO CREEK APACHE TEARS

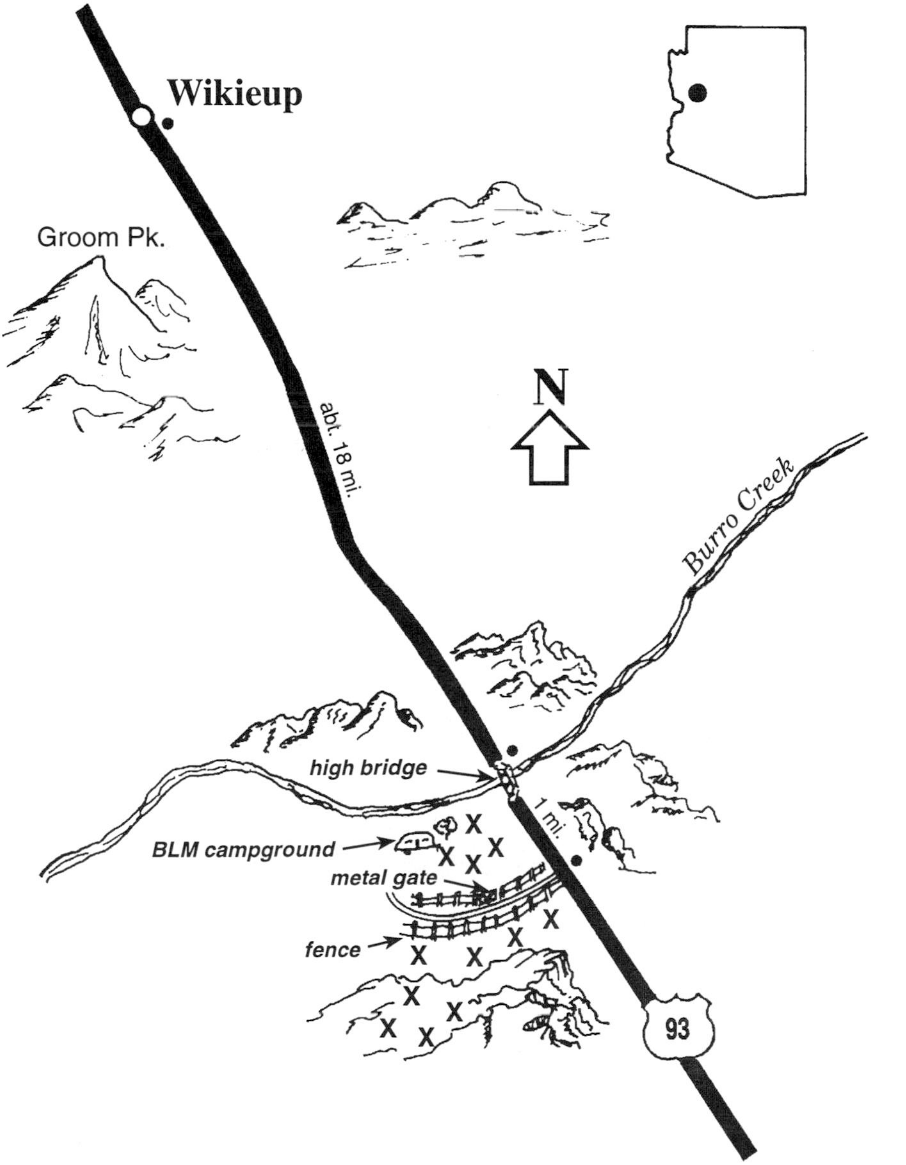

Wikieup

Groom Pk.

N

Burro Creek

abt. 18 mi.

high bridge

BLM campground

metal gate

fence

1 mi.

93

TO WICKENBURG --- abt. 59 mi.

This is not a new hunting area but it is easy to get to and seems to pay off every time. In fact, just about every rainstorm unearths a new supply of beautiful quartz crystals.

The turnoff is one and three-tenths miles past where Alamo Road intersects Highway 93, as shown on the map. You should proceed east at the sign designating Date Creek Ranch Road. Follow the graded dirt road about two and one-half miles to the edge of the mountains. At that point, there will be some ruts to the right. Follow the ruts a short distance farther to where signs of previous campfires can be seen. This marks the parking area.

Examine all terrain, starting from the campfire rings and continuing well into the foothills. As you proceed, numerous pits will be spotted, designating where past collectors have searched for the beautiful little gems. Single crystals and clusters can be found just about anywhere on the surface. The best tends to be obtainable only by strenuous digging with pick and shovel and/or using sledge hammers, chisels and gads in an attempt to open crystal filled cavities concealed within the native rock. Use existing pits for indications on where to start your own excavations.

Nice scepter crystals are said to have come from this renown location, but they are few and far between. Maybe you will be lucky enough to find one. There is also lots of bright white milky quartz scattered all over and it might be of interest for use in landscaping.

Clear quartz crystals

DATE CREEK QUARTZ CRYSTALS

Some of the finest agate in all of central Arizona can be found in the hills and valleys surrounding Perkinsville. To get to the prime collecting region, go south on County Road 12 from where it intersects Perkinsville Road, as shown on the map. After having gone about six and one-half miles you will be in the center of the rockhounding area. From there, extending quite a distance in all directions, the hills are filled with colorful agate. It seems that the largest pieces have generally been picked up in the vicinity of the telephone lines and cattle guard, but don't neglect other spots along the road.

Perkinsville agate displays a variety of colors and patterns. The most highly prized is a delicate pink material, frequently filled with interesting inclusions. In addition, fine multicolored, banded agate can also be obtained, and, it too is highly desirable.

Be advised that there is lots of private ranchland in this part of Arizona. Do not trespass, without first getting permission to do so. The hills are full of agate. If you have the time, it might be fruitful to obtain consent to explore some of the private lands, especially if not satisfied with what can be picked up near the road and in open areas.

It is recommended, while in the area, that you continue to the old city of Jerome. Jerome was a copper mining town which, at one time, boasted over 15,000 inhabitants. It is situated high on the side of Cleopatra Hill and provides spectacular views of the Verde Valley and Mogollon Rim. The scenic old city is partially restored and accommodates many shops and a fascinating mining museum, all of which should make the trip worth the time.

Some agate from the Perkinsville Area

PERKINSVILLE AGATE

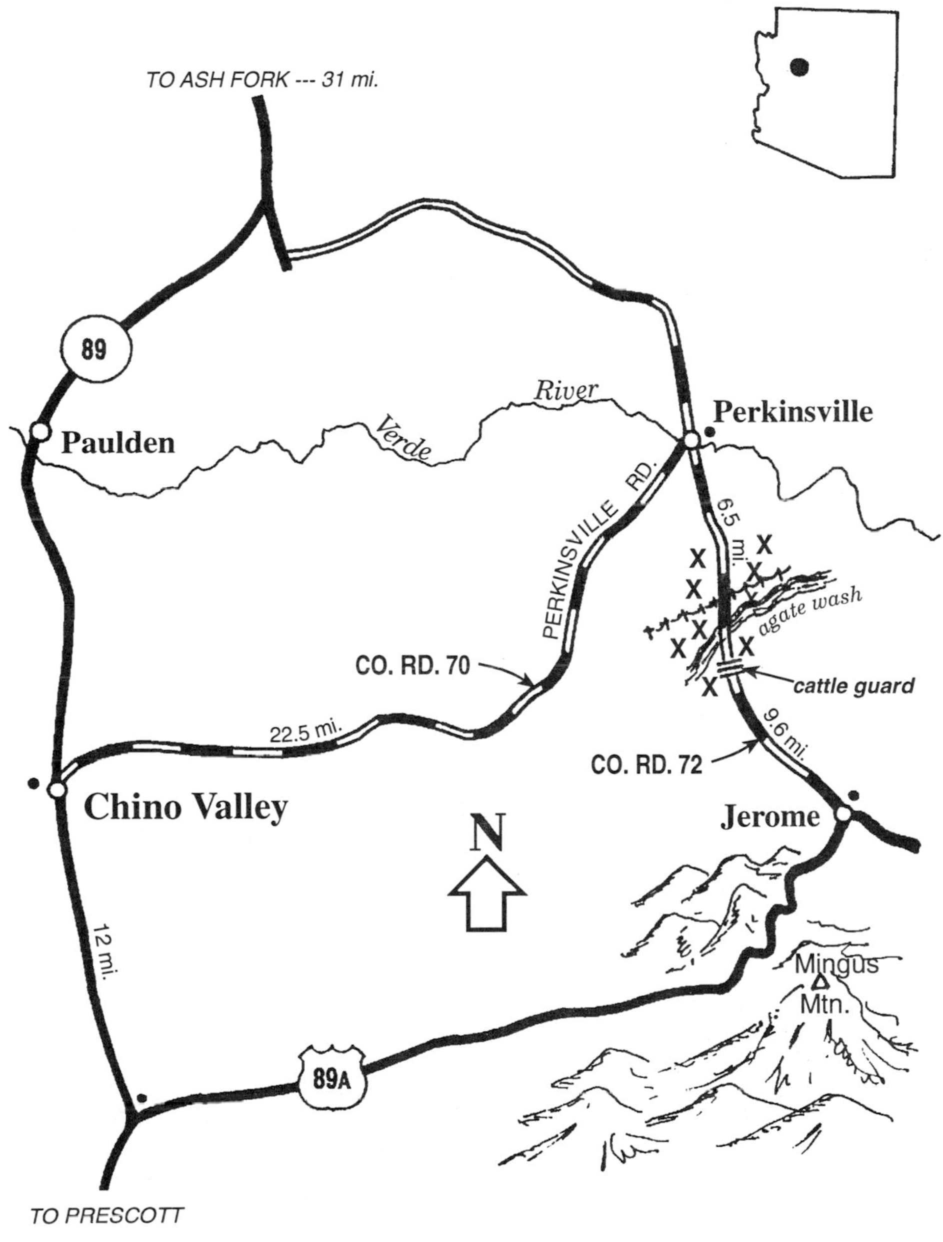

TO ASH FORK --- 31 mi.

89

Paulden

Verde *River*

Perkinsville

PERKINSVILLE RD.

6.5 mi.

X X X
X X
X X X
X X
X

agate wash

CO. RD. 70

cattle guard

22.5 mi.

CO. RD. 72

9.6 mi.

Chino Valley

N

Jerome

12 mi.

Mingus
△
Mtn.

89A

TO PRESCOTT

In the middle of the nineteenth century, gold was discovered in the Bradshaw Mountains near the present site of Prescott. In the ensuing years, countless mines shafts were dug into the hills and their associated dumps can still be seen scattered throughout the pine covered landscape.

These dumps often contain a wide variety of well-formed mineral specimens, including iron pyrite, chalcopyrite, malachite, chrysocolla, bornite, galena, hematite, sphalerite, quartz, and calcite, just to name a few. The pyrite can often be especially nice since it sometimes occurs in bright white quartz giving the appearance of gold. Be advised that some of the dumps are part of currently operating and/or privately owned mines, and should therefore not be explored unless permission has been obtained. The majority, however, are abandoned and thereby open to collecting.

The accompanying map shows a few of the more productive mine dumps in the region, all of which have potential for providing collectors an opportunity to find mineral specimens. Plan to take some time to rummage through the debris and split suspect stones to properly ascertain exactly what is hidden by their discolored and weathered surfaces. Frequently, you will break open an otherwise common appearing stone to find it filled with sparkling metallic crystals.

Be sure to wear goggles when cracking rocks, do not enter any shafts, and do not trespass onto any privately owned mine dump. Those illustrated on the accompanying map were accessible at the time of publication, but land status, especially in regard to gold mines, changes rapidly. If there is any doubt, move on and collect elsewhere.

Parked next to one of the many dumps in the Prescott area

PRESCOTT MINERALS

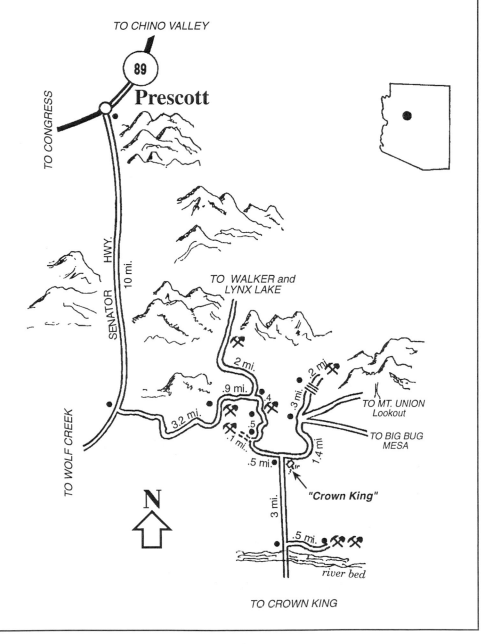

Copper Basin offers rockhounds the opportunity to gather a number of prized minerals, including beautiful blue azurite, green malachite, cuprite, molybdenite, quartz crystals, and even gold.

The entire region illustrated on the accompanying map, however, is privately owned by the Phelps Dodge Company. Their consent must be granted before you pick up anything. Permission can generally be obtained by contacting the company's branch office in nearby Prescott. If you don't make advance arrangements, it will be necessary to find the caretaker and try to work something out with him. It should be emphasized that collecting status changes from time to time, depending upon what type mining is taking place. Advance inquiry is highly recommended. No fee is charged, but rockhounds are restricted to specific areas and a liability release must be signed.

Copper Basin provides an easy place to search. Most of the minerals are brightly colored, making them stand out against the native rock like neon lights. Much of what can be picked up, however, is somewhat porous, and takes only a fair polish. Be sure to take time to look for the most solid and thick specimens. Pieces with both azurite and malachite are especially desirable and make real prizes in a mineral collection or when polished.

Camping is not allowed on the Phelps Dodge property, but there are lots of side roads in the area which afford good spots to set up for the night.

The road leading to the caretaker's house

COPPER BASIN MINERALS

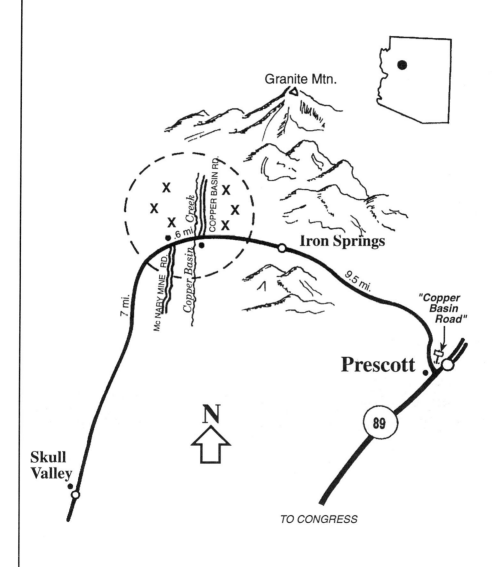

A vast onyx deposit is located just south of Interstate 40, a few miles west of Ash Fork. To get there, take the Crookton Road offramp, Exit 139. Follow the frontage road, which parallels the south side of the freeway, for approximately one and one-tenth miles. At that point, the main road veers off to the right, while the frontage road continues straight ahead. Proceed along the main tracks another two and eight-tenths miles, as illustrated on the map.

As you approach the given mileage, you will notice lots of the whitish-gray onyx strewn about. Starting at the provided mileage, and continuing all the way to the distant hills, there are numerous such onyx deposits, and each offers the potential for finding a variety of cutting material. Some is banded, especially that picked up nearer the mountains. Most, however, occurs in pastel shades of green, pink, gray, and white. The single color material is occasionally interesting, filled with fascinating patterns produced by ancient cracking and subsequent refilling. If you can get chunks of the "cracked" material, where the fissures have been completely filled with a contrasting hue, the polished results are nice.

There are lots of smaller pieces but most is somewhat weathered on the surface. If you have the time and energy, it could be worthwhile to do some hard rock work on any of the deposits themselves. The onyx is tough, and it takes lots of heavy labor, with sledge hammer, chisels, goggles and gloves, to remove sizable pieces. If you hit a good area, the dividends should compensate for the hard work.

There is lots of private ranch land in this region so be sure you do not collect in areas where trespassing is not allowed. Be sure, also, to leave all gates as you find them.

A view of the collecting site

CROOKTON ROAD ONYX

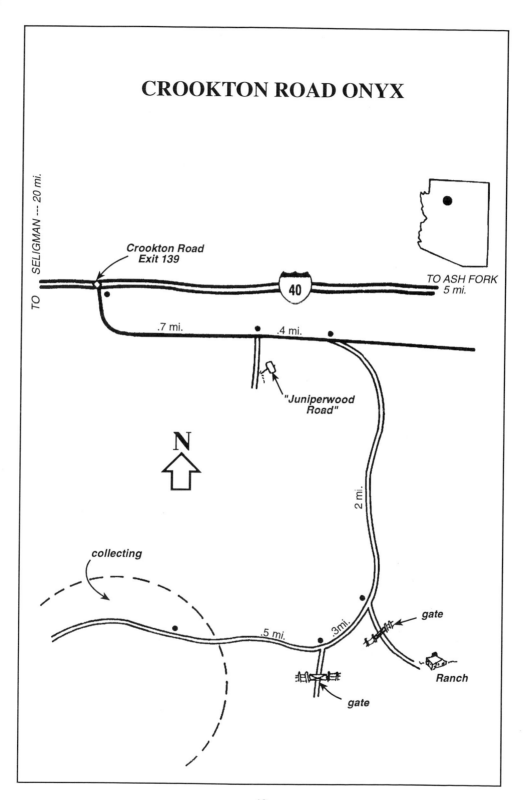

TO SELIGMAN --- 20 mi.

Crookton Road
Exit 139

40

TO ASH FORK
5 mi.

.7 mi.   .4 mi.

*"Juniperwood
Road"*

N

2 mi.

collecting

.5 mi.   .3mi.

gate

gate

Ranch

Lots of interestingly patterned sandstone, sometimes referred to as picture stone, can be obtained throughout the hills north of Ash Fork. In addition, fascinating little "volcanic bombs" can also be procured in the same general area.

To reach Site "A", the "volcanic bomb" spot, get on old Highway 66, as it goes through the center of town, and go north on First Street. Many of the street signs are no longer in place, so you might have to do a little exploration in order to locate this turn. It is on the east end of town, and there is a large church on the southwest corner, as illustrated on the map.

Go north, veer west, and then north again onto Double A Ranch Road. Continue on this paved thoroughfare three and one-half miles to Quarry Drive, bear right three-tenths of a mile, and then go right onto Lee Drive another three-tenths of a mile. At that point, turn right, go a short distance, and park. The little "volcanic bombs" are scattered all over the terrain and some make interesting display pieces for mineral collections.

To get to the picture stone area, return to Double A Ranch Road, double back south one and four-tenths miles to Canyon Road, and head northeast three and eight-tenths miles to Site "B". A rugged vehicle is suggested, especially if the road is wet. At the given mileage, you will find yourself traveling through a little pass in the foothills and the ground is covered with blocky, reddish-orange rock, which is the picture stone. Most is somewhat plain and it takes patient searching and splitting of suspect rock to obtain the best available.

Just west of the road is a little quarry where collectors have had some success, again by splitting the stone. This material is known locally as Flagstone and is commercially mined for use in decorative construction and landscaping.

Parked at the picture stone deposit

ASH FORK PICTURE STONE

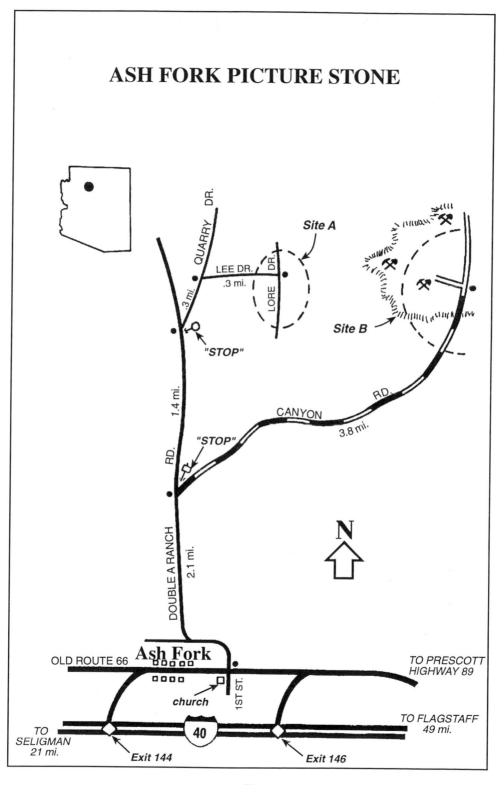

Fine samples of iron pyrite, chalcopyrite, feldspar, mica, chrysocolla, galena, hematite, malachite, pyromorphite, sphalerite, quartz crystals, and even gold, can be found in the many abandoned mine dumps near Crown King, situated high in the Bradshaw Mountains. In fact, even if the region didn't boast such good collecting, a drive up the well-graded, winding road would make the trip worthwhile. The views are often breathtaking, and the scenery is pristine.

To get to Crown King, take the well-marked offramp from Interstate 17 (Exit 259), three miles south of Cordes Junction. Continue west on the dirt road to the base of the mountains, about ten miles from the highway. Along the way, you will pass through the remnants of the old town of Cleator. Some good specimens can be obtained on the Cleator dumps, as well as on just about any other dump you encounter from that point on. Use a pick and shovel for digging. Be prepared to split suspect stones with a sledge hammer and chisel in order to properly ascertain exactly what treasures might be hidden by their often weathered surfaces.

Continue approximately twelve more miles up the steep winding road to Crown King. The hills surrounding Crown King are dotted with old mines, and, as mentioned earlier, just about any of them provides good collecting potential. One of the best known is the Fat Jack, located about five miles south of town. It is strongly suggested that you only visit the Fat Jack if you have a four-wheel drive vehicle, since the road is quite rough and rutted, in places.

The Fat Jack is noted for its beautiful quartz crystals, which are found in veins within the host schist. Some of the crystals exhibit beautiful purple amethyst hues and frequently occur as scepters. Although uncommon, there have been reports of mud filled cavities literally filled with sparkling specimens. Those are few and far between, and lots of luck, as well as persistence, is required in order to find such cavities.

Do not, under any circumstances, enter any shafts, since most are very rotten and dangerous. Be sure you do not gather minerals from valid mining claims. Only collect on dumps where it is allowed.

CROWN KING MINERALS

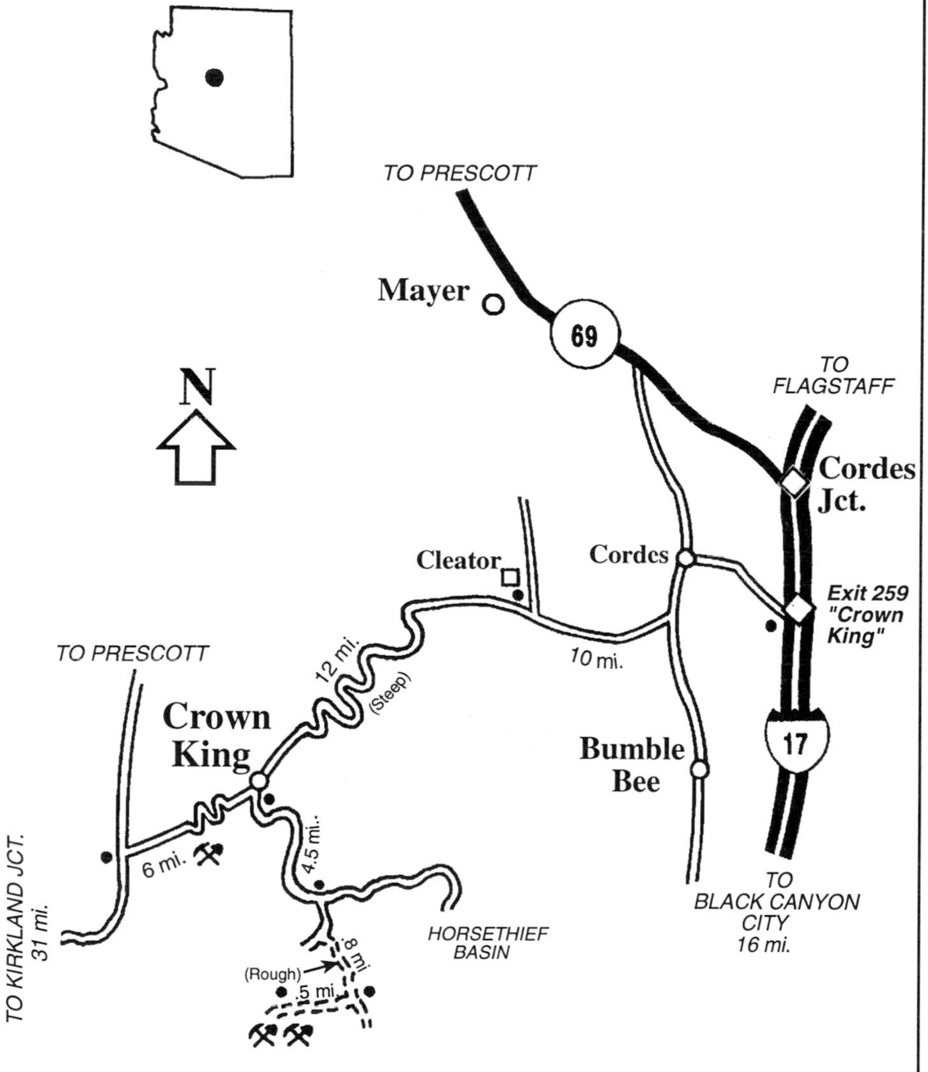

N

TO PRESCOTT

Mayer

69

TO FLAGSTAFF

Cordes Jct.

Cleator

Cordes

Exit 259 "Crown King"

TO PRESCOTT

12 mi.

(Steep)

10 mi.

Crown King

Bumble Bee

17

6 mi.

4.5 mi.

TO KIRKLAND JCT. 31 mi.

.8 mi.

(Rough)

.5 mi.

HORSETHIEF BASIN

TO BLACK CANYON CITY 16 mi.

Gem quality obsidian can be found scattered throughout an extensive area north of Parks. To get to this highly productive and scenic location, take Interstate 40 to Exit 178, about seventeen miles west of Flagstaff. Go seven-tenths of a mile to the town of Parks, and then proceed north on Spring Valley Road, which is also Forest Road 141. The pavement ends after four and three-tenths miles, but the dirt road is well maintained and should not present a problem, even to average clearance passenger cars, as long as it is dry.

Continue another two and nine-tenths miles and turn right onto Forest Road 107, driving an additional one and six-tenths miles to where a road intersects on the left. Obsidian Tank can be seen a short distance further, on the right. You will be able to spot the jet-black obsidian even before getting out of your vehicle, since it is scattered everywhere.

The quality varies considerably, with some being opaque, but most does possess some degree of transparency. The most suitable for faceting and other lapidary applications is free of internal inclusions, dark black, and nearly transparent. There is also some intriguing banded and swirled material which is also desirable.

Interesting little limb casts can be picked up, but they are rare. In addition, there is lots of limestone and some contains tiny fossils.

This is primarily a summer, late spring, and early fall collecting spot, since much of the region is covered with snow during the winter. Be advised, though, that the summer often brings severe afternoon thunderstorms which can make the dirt roads dangerous for driving in any but the most rugged of vehicles. If you want to spend some time, the entire locality surrounding Obsidian Tank offers a great place to camp, situated within the national forest, among the beautiful pine trees.

View of the collecting area and Obsidian Tank

PARKS OBSIDIAN

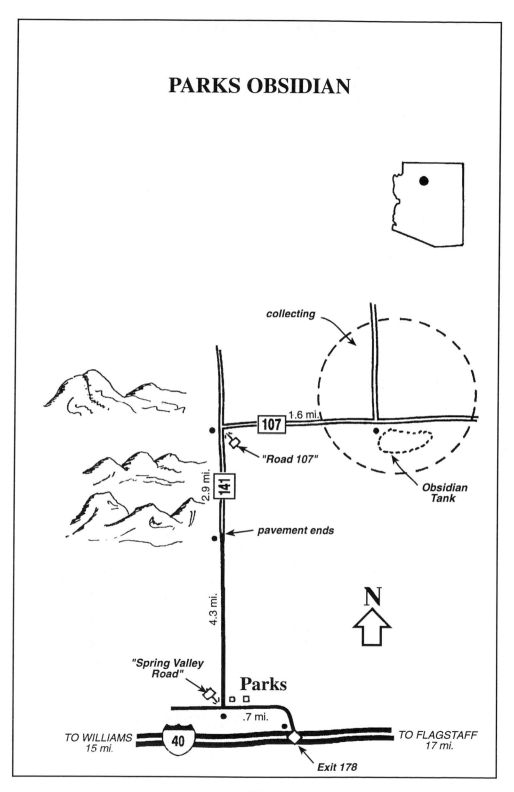

collecting

107 1.6 mi.

"Road 107"

141 2.9 mi.

Obsidian Tank

pavement ends

4.3 mi.

N

"Spring Valley Road"

Parks

.7 mi.

TO WILLIAMS
15 mi.

40

TO FLAGSTAFF
17 mi.

Exit 178

The old salt mine west of Camp Verde has long been known among Arizona rockhounds. Excellent crystallized specimens of halite, glauberite, gypsum, calcite, aragonite and kyanite can be found there, as well as a host of lesser known minerals.

To get to this fascinating and productive location from Camp Verde, head south out of town about four-tenths of a mile to Salt Mine Road and turn right. Continue one and one-half miles. As you proceed, a brilliant white hill will be spotted in the west, which marks the salt mine. As you drive past the hill, there is a little road leading toward it which should be followed to the gate, only a short distance away. At that point, park and hike into the salt area. Be advised that this location is privately owned, but town officials advise that collectors are allowed onto the property as long as they take only a limited number of specimens and do not enter any of the dangerous shafts.

It is advisable to wear sun glasses when collecting here, since the glare from the white salt is blinding on a sunny day. In addition, be careful when digging into the hill, since it is easy to damage the delicate crystals with a carelessly placed shovel. Hand tools are much more appropriate. Look for crystals growing out of the soil and carefully dig them out. Some will exhibit beautiful crystal surfaces, making outstanding additions for a collection.

Colorful agate can be found throughout the region surrounding Brown Springs, about eighteen miles farther south. To get there, follow Forest Road 574, as illustrated on the map. Be advised, however, that the road is very rough in places and it is essential that your vehicle is capable of making such a trip. If you decide to go, it is suggested that you take along some extra supplies in the event that you are delayed.

View of the collecting area

CAMP VERDE AREA

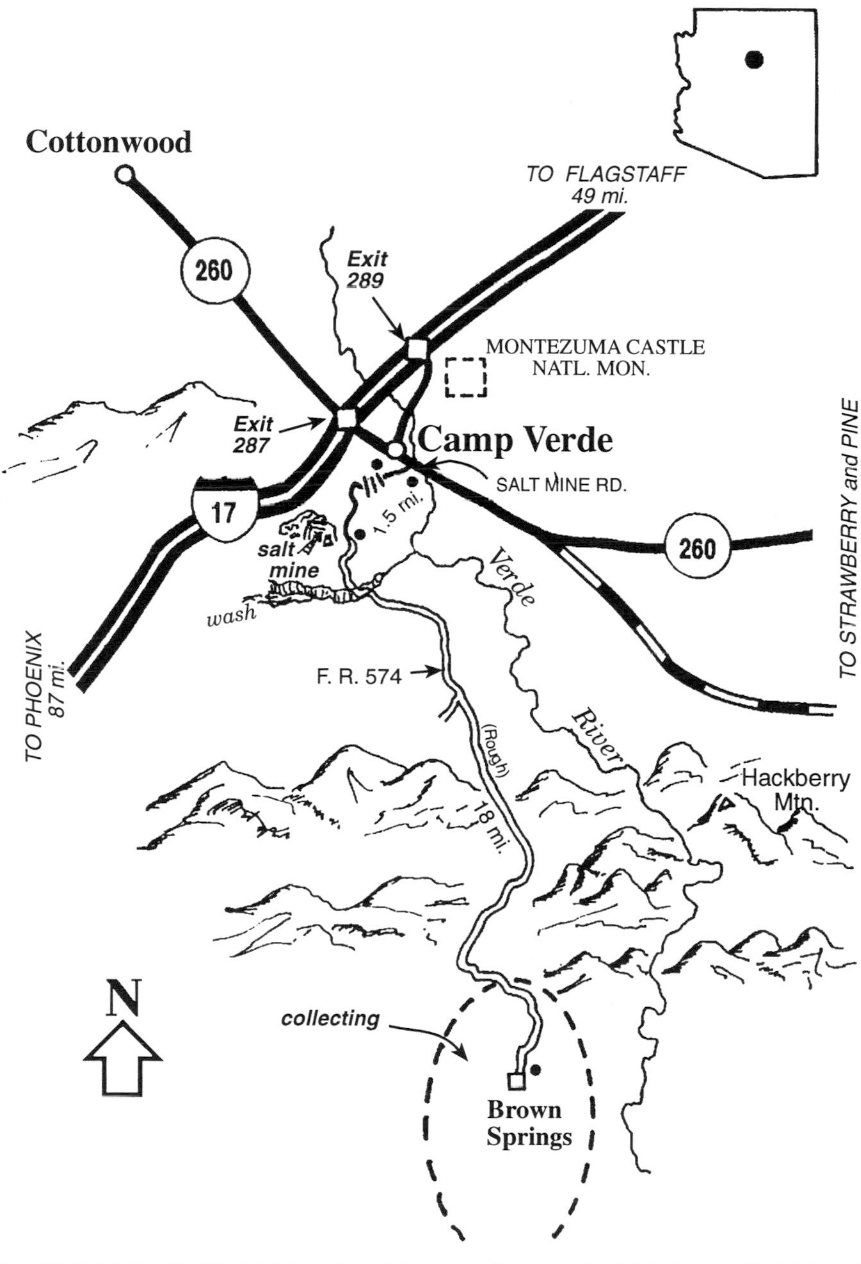

Cottonwood

TO FLAGSTAFF
49 mi.

260

Exit
289

MONTEZUMA CASTLE
NATL. MON.

Exit
287

Camp Verde

SALT MINE RD.

17

1.5 mi.

salt
mine

260

wash

TO STRAWBERRY and PINE

F. R. 574

Verde

TO PHOENIX
87 mi.

(Rough)

River

18 mi.

Hackberry
Mtn.

N

collecting

Brown
Springs

Interesting but small, specimens of fossilized coral can be found on a hill just off Highway 87, a short distance north of Payson. To get there, head north from town five and one-tenth miles to the bridge, which crosses the East Verde River. From that point, go exactly nine-tenths of a mile and turn left. A stop sign and cattle guard helps make the turnoff easy to spot. There is also a little grave, surrounded by a white picket fence, at the far end of the clearing. Park anywhere near the grave and carefully cross the busy highway.

Once on the east side of the road, carefully examine all rock you encounter, looking for the coral. At first, it looks like little "eyes" or holes filling the stone. Upon closer examination, the ridges indicative of coral can easily be discerned. For some reason, the first piece is always the toughest to find. Once you discover your first specimen, subsequent coral should be easier to spot. Don't expect to gather huge quantities, though, since everything tends to be quite small. It is sometimes worthwhile to take along a hand sledge to break off portions of suspect stones, in hopes of exposing otherwise concealed coral.

Allow plenty of time to adequately explore the hillside, and don't hesitate to do some hiking, especially on the eastern side of the highway fence. Be aware, that the hill is covered with thorny bushes and they have the potential for making it a painful place.

Specimens are much too porous to be polished, but, if you can find a rare, sizable piece which contains lots of the coral, it can be great for display in a collection. This is definitely a location that requires lots of patience, but the search isn't difficult, and the site is extremely accessible.

Fossil corral filled rock found at the site

EAST VERDE FOSSILS

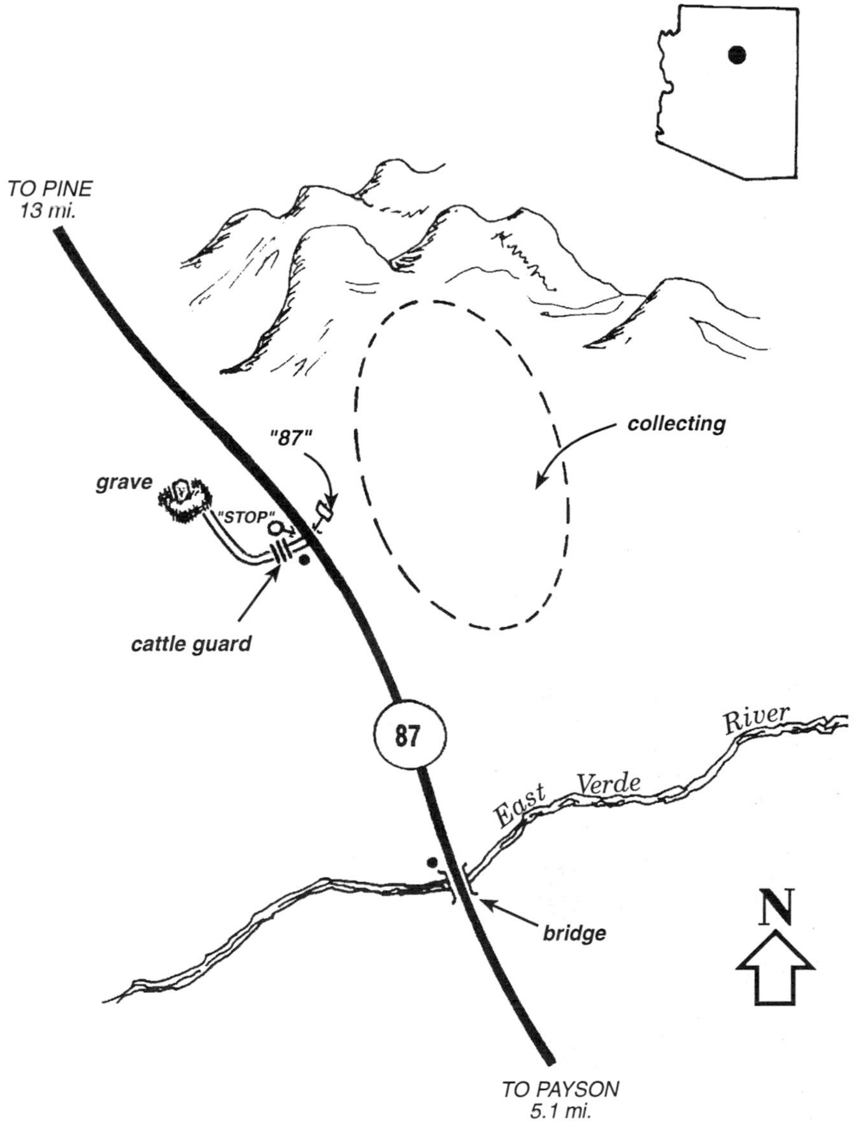

TO PINE
13 mi.

"87"

collecting

grave

"STOP"

cattle guard

87

River

East Verde

bridge

N

TO PAYSON
5.1 mi.

Deep red jasper can be found strewn randomly throughout the pine trees near Black Canyon Lake. To get there, go two and nine-tenths miles east from the small town of Forest Lakes, on Highway 260. At that point, Forest Road 300 intersects from the south, and it is there were you should turn. The intersection is easy to spot, and there is a sign designating it to be the road to Black Canyon Lake and Gentry Lookout Tower. It is difficult to find a safe place to double back and try again if you miss the turn, so be alert.

Drive along Forest Road 300 about eight-tenths of a mile to where a primitive campground will be encountered on the left. This offers a great place to spend a night, and, at time of publication, there was no charge to stay there.

The red jasper is scattered in all directions from the campground, for quite a distance, but the quality varies considerably. The larger pieces tend to be very grainy and more maroon in color, rather than the desirable fire engine red. It shouldn't take too long before you can gather samples of the good solid red material, most of which is only pebble-size, but suitable for tumbling, beads, and smaller cabochons. There are some larger chunks, however, so just be patient and willing to walk to less accessible places. Generally, the more vivid the red, the more solid the jasper.

The major challenge encountered at this location is presented by the ever present pine needles which cover so much of the ground. As a consequence, the most productive places to search are in clearings, such as within the campground or on the graded roads. There is plenty of jasper hidden under the pine needles, but, without doing some heavy raking, that material will probably never be found. A good time to visit is shortly after a heavy rain, where new material might be exposed and/or cleaned, making it much easier to spot.

View of the collecting area

BLACK CANYON RED JASPER

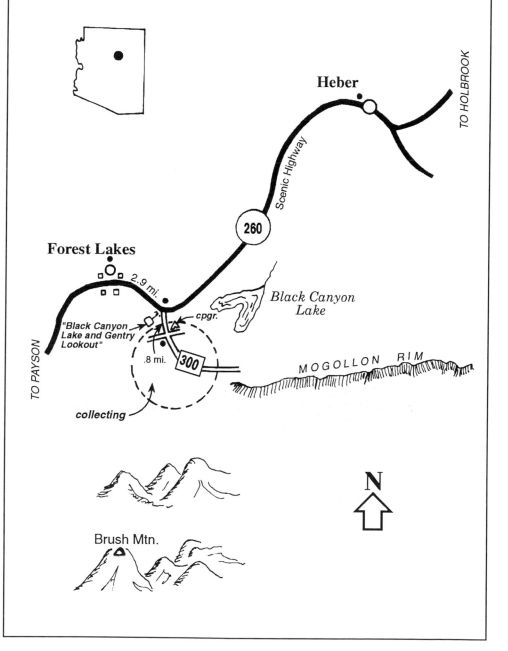

TO HOLBROOK

Heber

Scenic Highway

260

Forest Lakes

2.9 mi.

Black Canyon
Lake

cpgr.

"Black Canyon
Lake and Gentry
Lookout"

MOGOLLON RIM

TO PAYSON

.8 mi.

300

collecting

N

Brush Mtn.

This location offers geodes, nodules, and occasional chunks of agate, and it doesn't take long to gather nice specimens of each. To get there, take Forest Road 64 about twelve miles west from Highway 260, as shown on the map. The turnoff is well graded and easy to spot, since there is a sign designating it to also be the route to Tonto Village. If you reach the East Verde River bridge, you have gone too far and should double back exactly one mile. Partially overgrown ruts will be seen leading up the hillside at the given mileage. Park near where they intersect and hike to the upper ridge, about fifty yards away.

The interesting "bubbly" little orbs are found lying on the surface, on either side of the ruts. There is another somewhat weathered road, paralleling Forest Road 64, about fifty yards up the hillside. It is literally paved with geodes and nodules for quite a distance, in both directions. Inspect ravines, hillsides and areas of erosion, or rake through the pine needles to expose otherwise hidden specimens. Digging isn't really necessary, but a small shovel or pick would be helpful for removing specimens that have become partially embedded in the hard packed soil.

Size varies greatly, ranging from those as small as peas to others over ten inches in diameter. The small ones are abundant, but grapefruit size samples are also fairly easy to find. For the most part, they have bubbly tan exteriors, but some are brown or nearly black. A large percentage of the Payson geodes do not contain crystal filled cavities, but they do make nice display pieces, uncut. In addition to the geodes, nice blue and white agate can also be found, some of which is of a very good quality.

Parked at the collecting location

PAYSON GEODES & NODULES

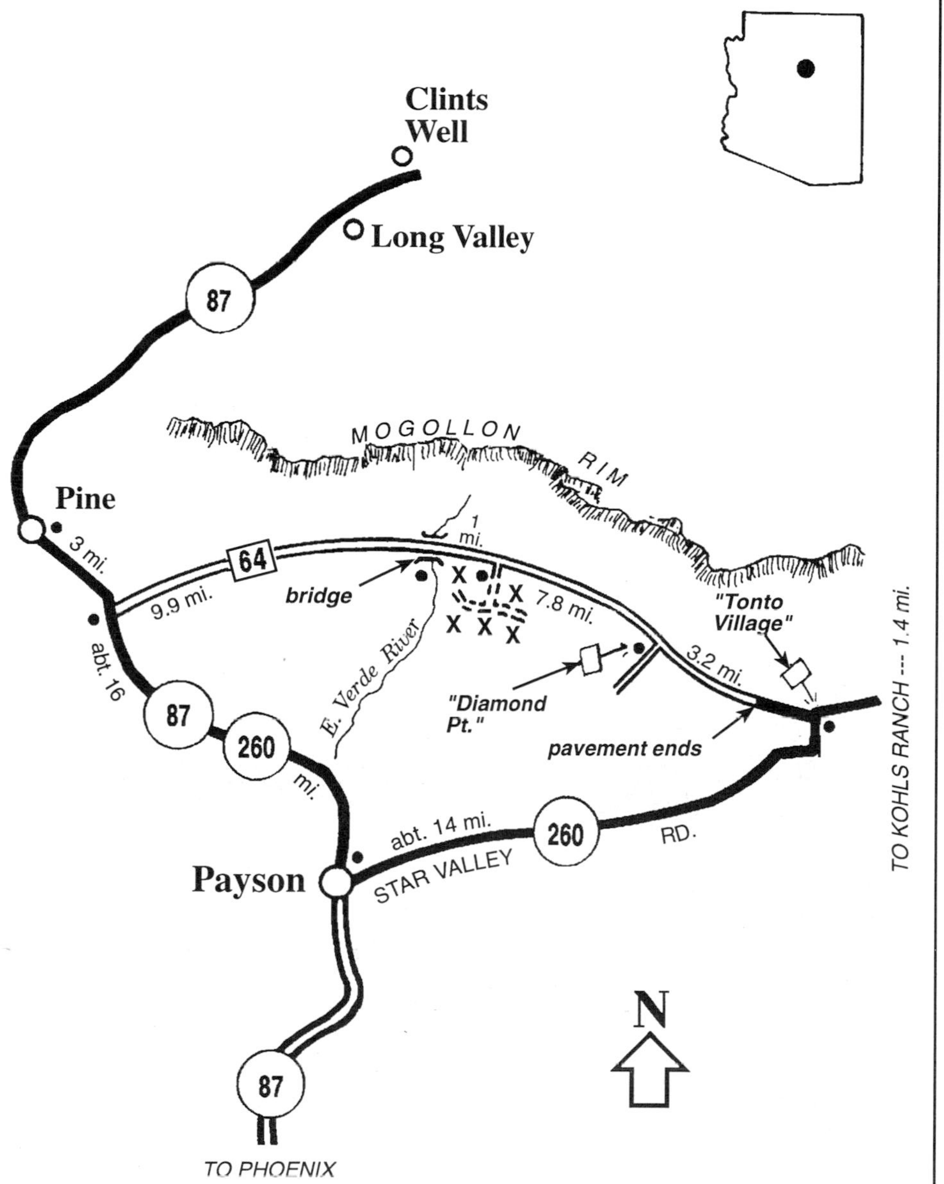

Clints
Well

Long Valley

87

MOGOLLON RIM

Pine

3 mi.

64

1 mi.

bridge

9.9 mi.

X · X
X X X
X X X   7.8 mi.

"Tonto
Village"

abt. 16

"Diamond
Pt."

3.2 mi.

87

260

pavement ends

E. Verde River

mi.

TO KOHLS RANCH --- 1.4 mi.

abt. 14 mi.   **260**   RD.

Payson

STAR VALLEY

87

TO PHOENIX

N

◆ ——— CHRISTOPHER CREEK JASPER ——— ◆

Interesting gray and white banded and swirled jasper can be found along the banks of scenic Christopher Creek, a short distance from Kohls Ranch. To get to this easily accessible spot, head from Kohls Ranch toward Heber, on Highway 260, about four miles to the Christopher Creek Picnic Area turnoff. Go about two-tenths of a mile to the picnic area, situated on the bank of Christopher Creek, and park. If you reach the tiny town of Christopher Creek, you have gone too far and should double back eight-tenths of a mile. The picnic area is a great place to stop for a snack or lunch, amid the trees, and the collecting area is just below, in the creek bed.

The unusual cutting material isn't too difficult to find. Once you get your first piece, and see exactly what you are looking for, subsequent chunks tend to be easier to obtain. To get to the best collecting, carefully scramble down the bank from the picnic area into the rocky creek bed. Some of the rocks can be slick, so be sure you have good footing, especially in wet areas. There is lots of small material scattered throughout the rubble. Larger pieces are usually found by walking farther down the creek or by breaking off chunks of larger rock with a sledge hammer or rock pick, in hopes of exposing otherwise hidden regions of the swirled jasper.

The best is milky brown with contrasting white bands and swirls. Material with good color saturation and contrast produce the best polished pieces. Most is large enough to make sizable cabochons or other lapidary items, and if you are willing to spend sufficient time, you should be very satisfied with what can be found. Additional specimens of this most unusual material can be gathered throughout the region, but this is, by far, the most accessible.

Swirled jasper from the Christopher Creek area

Exploring the jasper bearing wash

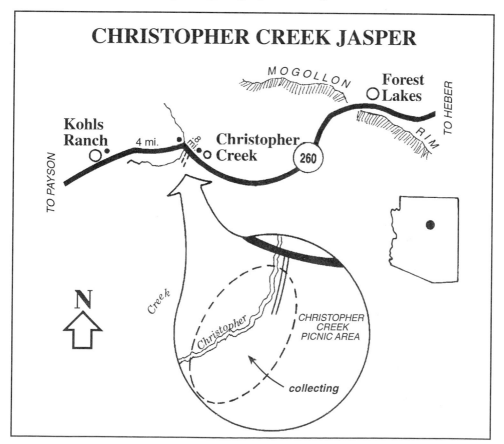

CHRISTOPHER CREEK JASPER

MOGOLLON

Forest
Lakes

TO HEBER

Kohls
Ranch

4 mi.

Christopher
Creek

260

RIM

TO PAYSON

N

Creek

Christopher

CHRISTOPHER
CREEK
PICNIC AREA

collecting

This is good summer hunting area, situated in the cool pine trees, a short distance from the Mogollon Rim. The quartz crystals found at Diamond Point are frequently very clear and many are doubly terminated, often resembling New York's highly prized Herkimer diamonds.

To reach the area, follow Highway 260, Star Valley Road, from Payson about fourteen miles to Forest Road 64. This is a well-maintained, national forest access road, and there is a sign at the intersection designating it to be the road to Tonto Village. Go west four and two-tenths miles, turn south onto Forest Road 65, and continue another three and four-tenths miles. At that point, pull off the road and park. There are some great places to camp in and around Diamond Point, and the view is spectacular.

This spot has been known for years and, for that reason, most of the surface crystals have been picked up. Heavy rainstorms, however, never fail to expose additional specimens on or near the road for quite a distance in all directions. Productive pockets can also be found by hiking from where you park toward the fence overlooking the cliff. You will see where previous rockhounds have worked before. and, with a little chipping, sifting and digging, it shouldn't be too difficult to expose some of the tiny little gems.

Generally, the most productive method for gathering the elusive crystals is to work with gads, chisels and hammers on the boulders strewn throughout the area. This is hard work, but the rewards are usually worth it. If you don't feel like engaging in such tough labor, try some shallow digging and sifting of the loose soil near the white and orange quartz outcrops. It takes patience to find Diamond Point crystals, but their quality makes the effort worthwhile.

Parked at the collecting site

DIAMOND POINT CRYSTALS

TO HIGHWAY 87 --- 23 mi.

MOGOLLON RIM

64

Christopher Creek

"Tonto Village"

3.4 mi.

65

4.2 mi.

TO HEBER --- 31 mi.

1.4 mi.

Diamond Point

X
X X

fire lookout tower

Kohls Ranch

87

260

STAR VALLEY RD.

abt. 14 mi.

Payson

N

TO PHOENIX

◆ ———— WOODRUFF PETRIFIED WOOD ———— ◆

If you would like to gather specimens of petrified wood similar to that protected within the boundaries of Petrified Forest National Park, there is a fine place to do so a short distance south of Holbrook, near the small town of Woodruff. Most of what can be found is not too large, but great for making cabochons and for tumbling.

To get there, take Highway 77 south from Holbrook about six and one-half miles and then turn left toward Woodruff. From that point, heading east all the way to Silver Creek, on both sides of the road, one can pick up pieces of the spectacularly colored wood. The most prolific concentration, however, is about three to four miles from Highway 77. There, chunks of the highly prized material seem to be scattered just about everywhere. There is a little hill, on the south side of the road, three and one-half miles from Highway 77 which provides a good place from which to base your search.

Size tends to be small, but there are a few larger specimens scattered about. In addition, one can find an occasional perfectly formed twig. This material is of the highest quality, and takes an outstanding polish. Colors include bright yellow, orange, red and white.

The area stretching about twenty miles south of Woodruff along the ranch road following Silver Creek is also a good hunting area. Be sure, however, to check for loose sand before pulling off any roads in this area. Also look for a fine variety of moss agate, while collecting near Woodruff.

Collecting along the road about three and one-half miles from Highway 77

WOODRUFF PETRIFIED WOOD

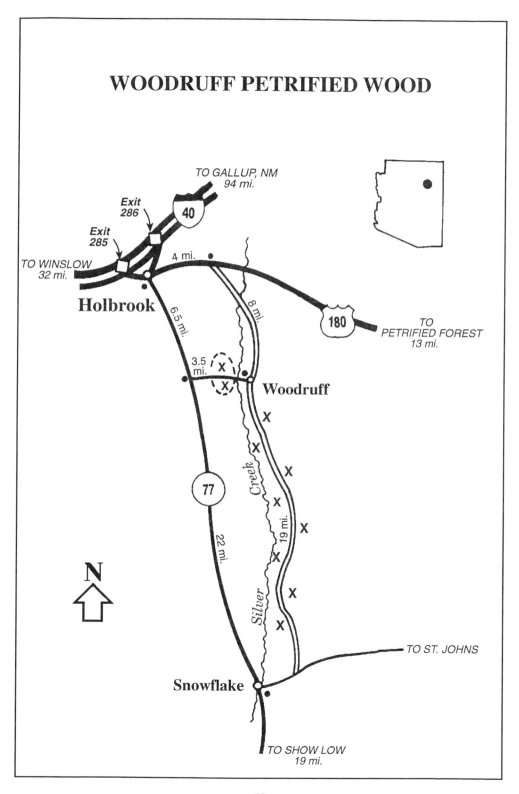

TO GALLUP, NM
94 mi.

Exit 286

Exit 285

40

TO WINSLOW
32 mi.

4 mi.

Holbrook

8 mi.

180

TO PETRIFIED FOREST
13 mi.

6.5 mi.

3.5 mi.

X

X

Woodruff

X

X

Creek

X

77

X

X

X

19 mi.

X

Silver

X

X

TO ST. JOHNS

Snowflake

TO SHOW LOW
19 mi.

N

Some of the most beautiful petrified wood in the entire world comes from a limited area near the town of Holbrook. If you would like to gather specimens of this prized material, similar to that found within the protected boundaries of Petrified Forest National Park, there are only a few places where that can be done. One such spot is a fee location, under the jurisdiction of the Petrified Forest Gift Shop, situated on the southwest edge of the Petrified Forest National Park. To get there from Holbrook, take Highway 180 approximately eighteen miles east to the turnoff to Petrified Forest National Park. After turning, the shop will be on your left. The shop is where you must register, receive detailed collecting information, and pay the fee.

It is strongly advised that arrangements be made ahead of time by calling (602) 524-3470, but the owners are fairly flexible with last minute requests, if they have someone on duty who can accompany you. The cost is hefty, with a $250 minimum, priced per pound, based on the color and quality of what is found. The "wood yard" at the shop is filled with material from the collecting site, in much smaller and affordable quantities. Most people are very satisfied doing their "rockhounding" there, rather that engaging in the very difficult digging required to find their own.

The minimum fee is required in order to restrict entry to people who are genuinely interested in gathering petrified wood and not just wanting to do some off road driving throughout the ranch. If you pick up more than you want, it isn't necessary to take it all and if you do not quite get $250 worth, you can obtain the balance at the store.

Camping is allowed on property near the shop, and there is a graveled area upon which you can park a trailer or motorhome. There is no charge to stay there, but facilities and supplies are very limited.

Petrified logs

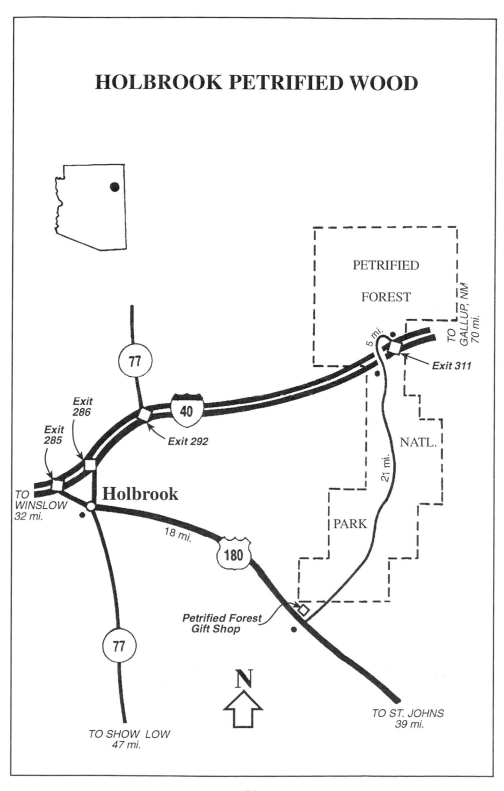

HOLBROOK PETRIFIED WOOD

PETRIFIED

FOREST

TO GALLUP, NM 70 mi.

5 mi.

Exit 311

77

Exit 286

40

Exit 292

Exit 285

NATL.

TO WINSLOW 32 mi.

21 mi.

Holbrook

18 mi.

PARK

180

Petrified Forest Gift Shop

77

N

TO ST. JOHNS 39 mi.

TO SHOW LOW 47 mi.

Sizable specimens of petrified wood can be found throughout the hills east of Joseph City. One of the most accessible areas is reached by taking Exit 277 from Interstate 40 and bearing right three-tenths of a mile. From there, there is a power line road which you should follow north about one-half mile, then turn right to the top of the little hill, about one-tenth of a mile farther.

From the moment you step out of your vehicle, you will see petrified wood littering the hills. Hike into the valley, and limb sections can be found. The Joseph City wood is not as colorful as that found near Holbrook and Woodruff. It occurrs for the most part in shades of gray and tan, but some is colorful, generally in solid tones. Some contains agate and opal seams, and these are often very desirable for use as display pieces. In addition, there is lots of brilliant yellow material with vivid red stringers, but beware that much of it is crumbly and/or easily fractured, so take time to be selective.

Extensive collecting has taken place here in recent years, especially near the road. At one time, this was a virtual petrified forest, with stumps and limbs protruding throughout the soft soil. Colossal specimens can still be found, but generally in more remote and less accessible regions. If you choose to explore outlying spots beyond the road, be certain you have a high-clearance, four-wheel drive vehicle, since the soil is loose and it is very easy to get stuck.

Before getting too carried away with your collecting, be sure to review government restrictions limiting quantities of petrified wood that any single person can take from public lands. These are outlined in the introduction.

In addition to the wood, this site also boasts nice agate and jasper in a variety of color and pattern combinations.

The road leading through the collecting area

JOSEPH CITY PETRIFIED WOOD

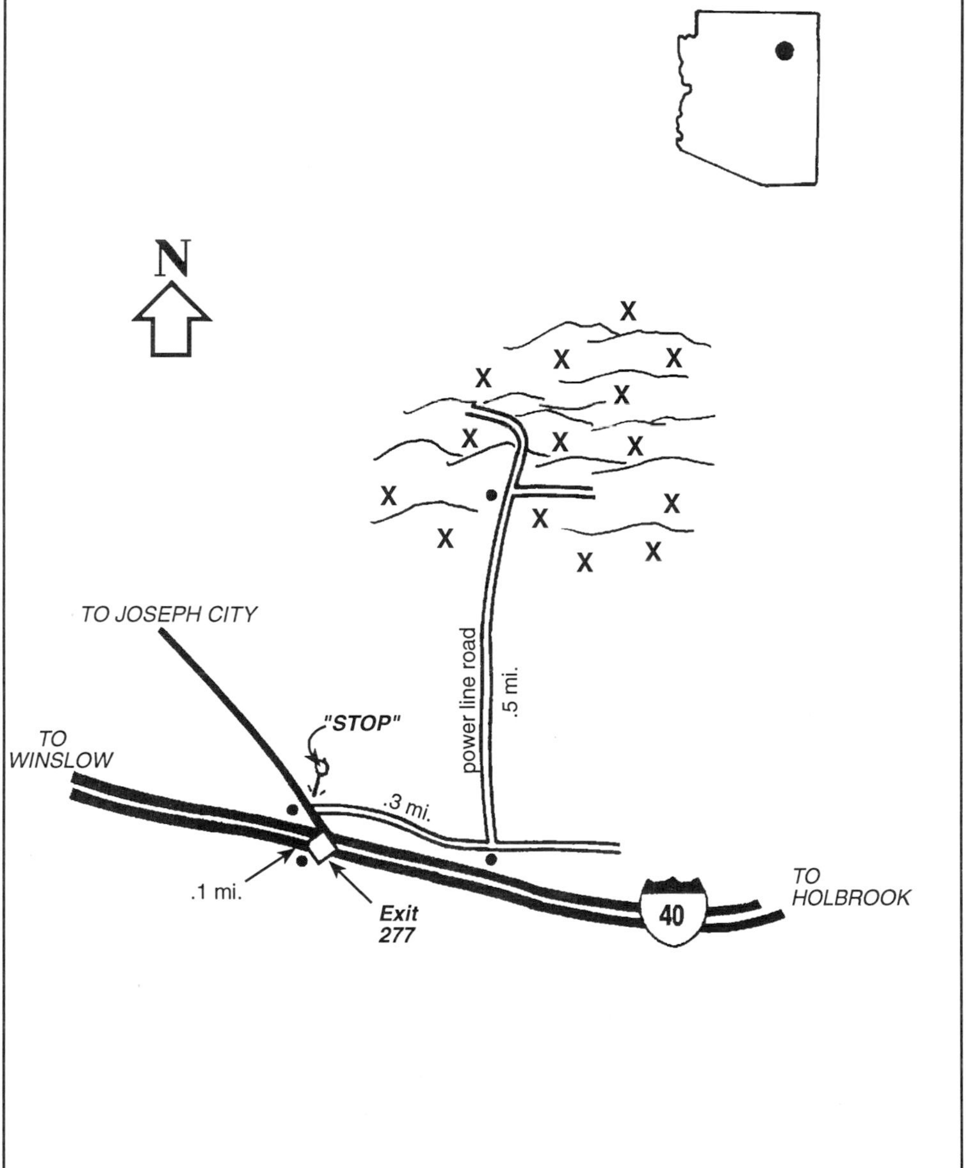

TO JOSEPH CITY

TO WINSLOW

"STOP"

power line road

.5 mi.

.3 mi.

.1 mi.

Exit 277

40

TO HOLBROOK

Colorful specimens of Arizona petrified wood can be found a short distance south of Winslow. To get to there, take Highway 87 south from town one mile and go left onto Highway 99. Continue six and two-tenths miles, past Clear Creek Reservoir, to the road heading for Holbrook. Follow that graded dirt road east about two-tenths of a mile to the beginning of this most extensive collecting area. From there, and continuing at least twenty miles, petrified wood, agate, and jasper can be obtained in random concentrations.

The best method to collect here is to drive a short distance, park, get out and search the terrain. If you have little or no luck, drive a little farther and try again as concentrations do vary. At one stop you may find very little of interest and, rather than waste you time there, the next stop might afford a far better concentration. Another reason for making several stops along the road is that the quality and variety of what can be found differs from spot to spot. At one place you may find a good selection of agate, but little else, while a short distance farther down the road you might encounter beautiful rainbow petrified wood. Even the wood color seems to vary from place to place.

Most of the material found here is somewhat weathered and rounded on the surface, but the colors tend to be so vivid, that spotting even those specimens is not much of a problem. Quality, solidness, patterning, color variation, etc., though, may be more difficult to determine until the piece is dipped in water or tumbled.

Exploring for rocks south of Winslow

WINSLOW PETRIFIED WOOD

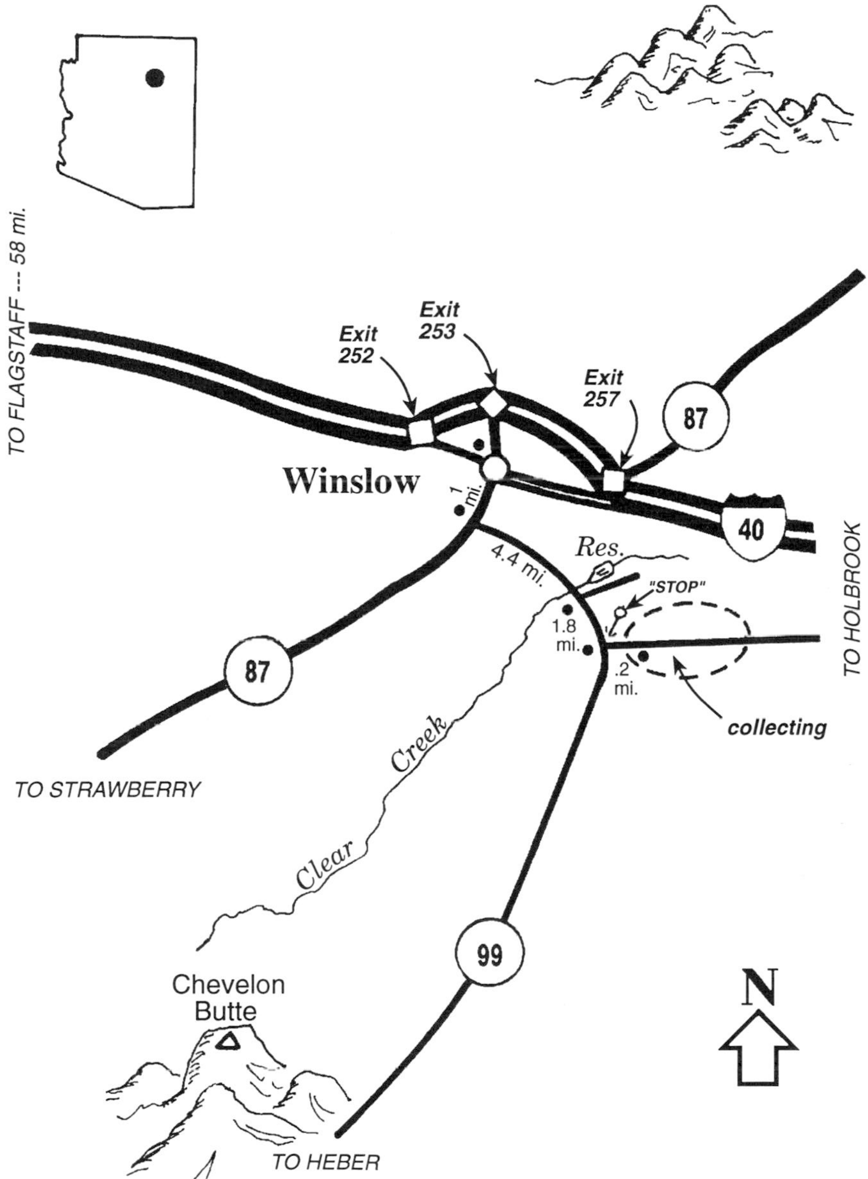

TO FLAGSTAFF --- 58 mi.

Exit 252

Exit 253

Exit 257

87

Winslow

40

1 mi.

4.4 mi.

Res.

"STOP"

1.8 mi.

.2 mi.

collecting

87

TO HOLBROOK

TO STRAWBERRY

Clear Creek

99

Chevelon Butte

TO HEBER

N

A most prolific place to gather good quality specimens of agate, jasper and petrified wood is within the vast region northeast of Winslow called Rincon Basin.

To get there, go east approximately ten miles on Interstate 40 from Winslow to the Hibbard Road exit, Exit 264. Drive north to the old frontage road and then double back west, four miles, to where tracks lead up a hill, on the right. The old frontage road is full of pot holes and is rough in places, but most passenger cars should be able to make the journey that far. From there, however, rugged vehicles and, in many cases, four-wheel drive units, may be required. If you don't have such transportation, it will probably be necessary to restrict your collecting to regions near the frontage road. That, though, is not a major problem, since lots can be found within easy walking distance.

Throughout the slopes of the little hill, and extending miles further north, the ground is littered with good collecting material. There is jasper, in a variety of vivid colors; agate, sometimes filled with interesting inclusions; nice bubbly chalcedony; pastel chert; and petrified wood, ranging from an uninteresting tan to some that is quite colorful. There is a cross and a little amphitheater on top of the hill, and the view is nice.

If you have time and a sense of adventure, be sure to set out and explore some of the roads and ruts which crisscross the northern regions. It is an interesting, mineral-rich place to investigate. The agate and jasper seem to be concentrated higher up, on the mesas and hilltops, while the wood tends to be in and around the lower, soft, gray mounds. All, however, can be found in the lowlands, due to erosion.

If you do choose to explore some of the more remote areas, be advised that the roads traverse loose sand and are rough and washed out in places. Be certain your vehicle is capable of traveling under such circumstances, since this would be a lonesome place to get stuck.

Searching for specimens

RINCON BASIN MINERALS

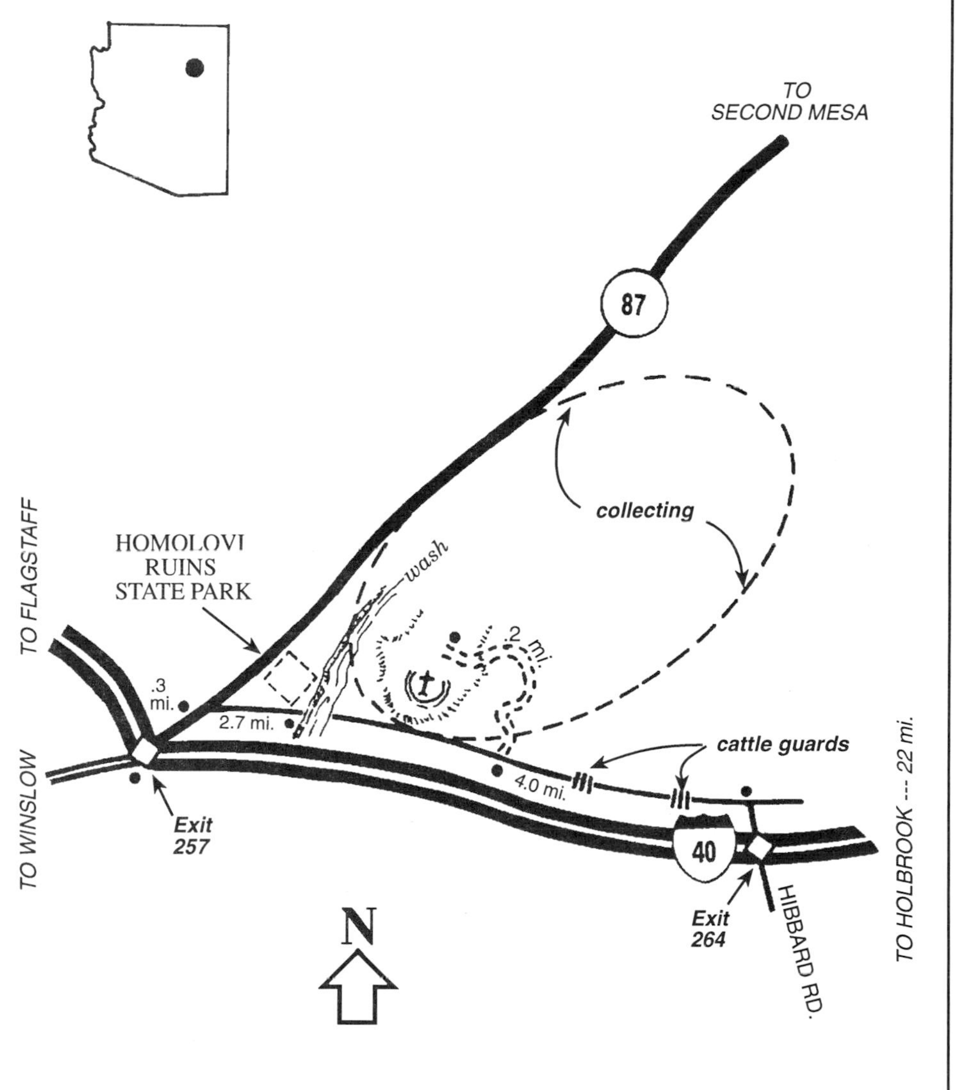

TO
SECOND MESA

87

TO FLAGSTAFF

HOMOLOVI
RUINS
STATE PARK

wash

collecting

.2 mi.

TO WINSLOW

.3
mi.

2.7 mi.

4.0 mi.

cattle guards

TO HOLBROOK --- 22 mi.

Exit
257

40

Exit
264

HIBBARD RD.

N

Not far from Salome are the remains of the once booming gold mining town of Harquahala. The associated dumps and sparse remnants of the townsite can still be visited. In addition, there are some nice mineral specimens available to the rockhound who is willing to spend some time digging through the rubble and rock piles.

The town began with the discovery of gold in 1888 by Harry Watton, Bob Stein and Mike Sullivan. Before the ore ran out, the total production was about $2,500,000. On the dumps, collectors can find fine specimens of red hematite, quartz, chrysocolla, malachite, dioptase, calcite, pyrite, chalcopyrite, galena, and even some delicate gypsum.

To get there, take Highway 60 to Salome and then turn onto the paved road heading south from the middle of town. Bear right onto Harquahala Mine Road, about one-tenth of a mile along the way, as shown on the map. Continue twelve miles on the graded dirt road and the dumps will be easily spotted on the hill. After having gone about five miles, and continuing intermittently as you proceed, a number of additional mine dumps will be seen. Any of them afford good collecting potential and, if they are abandoned, it might be worth your time to explore a few. If you choose to leave the main road, be certain your vehicle can negotiate the often washed out ruts.

When at the mines, be very careful, since there are lots of rusty nails and some broken glass. Some of the mining property may be fenced off and even worked with machinery. If the property is fenced or posted, do not enter without permission. In addition, do not enter any mine shaft, no matter how promising it might appear.

The Bonanza Mine offers additional collecting, and the dumps are located four and two-tenths miles north of nearby Wenden, as shown. You can find pyrite and other mineral specimens there, but the road is fairly rough, necessitating the use of rugged, high-clearance vehicles.

HARQUAHALA MINE MINERALS

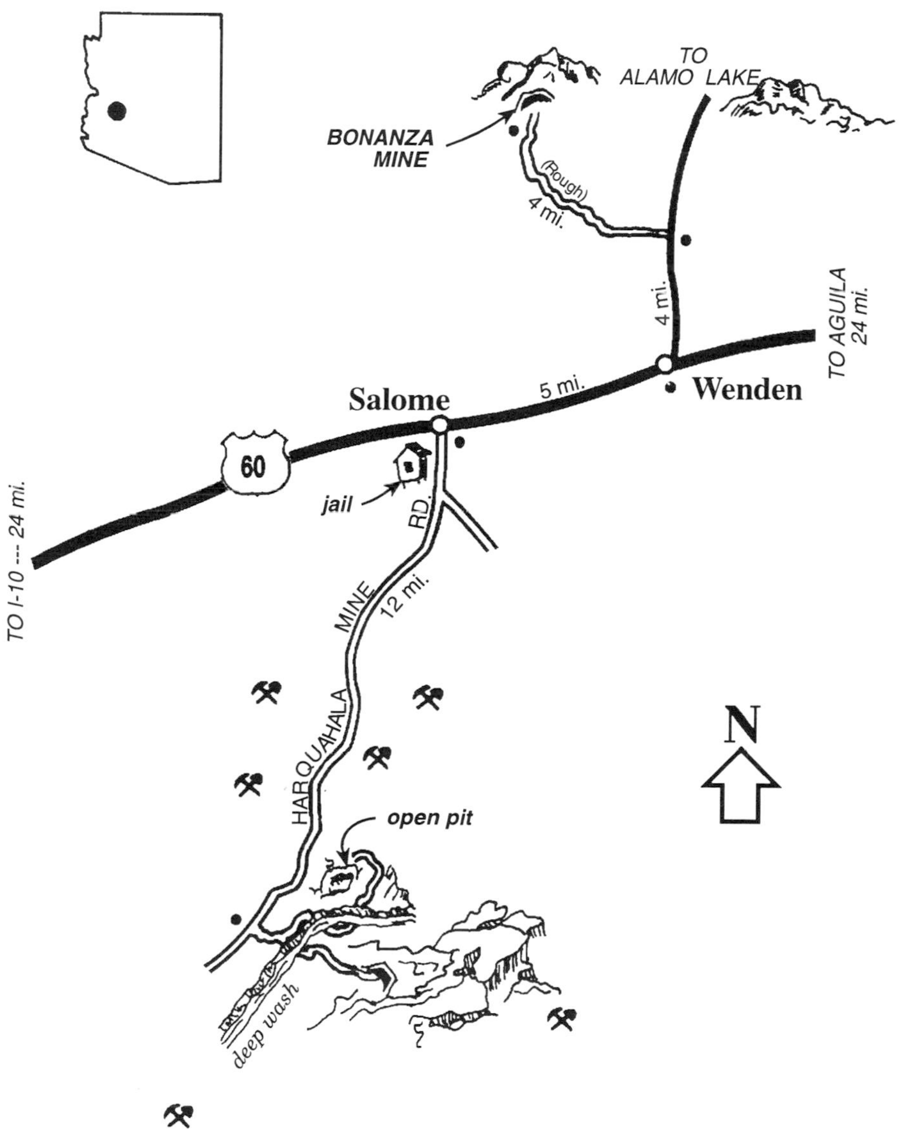

TO ALAMO LAKE

BONANZA MINE

(Rough) 4 mi.

TO AGUILA 24 mi.

4 mi.

Salome 5 mi. Wenden

60

jail

TO I-10 --- 24 mi.

HARQUAHALA MINE RD.

12 mi.

open pit

deep wash

N

Much of the material that can be found while rock collecting can be tumble polished. Tumbling is the form of stone polishing through which a large segment of rockhounds get into the gem hobby. It is a relatively easy craft which produces really beautiful gemstones that can be used in an almost endless variety of jewelry and decorator items. Once the "bug" has bitten you, you may well find yourself branching out into other types of gem cutting and jewelry making. Whatever route you follow, you can be assured you are going to spend many enjoyable, relaxing hours, and you will be able to turn out creations of striking beauty for personal use, gifts, and/or a profitable part-time business.

The following eqipment and supplies are needed to become involved in the craft of gemstone tumbling:

(1.) *Equipment.* Appropriately, the machine that is used is called a tumbler. There is a wide variety of tumblers available, and prices range from quite low to medium, for the most part.

(2.) *Rough gemstone material.* Many various types of stones are tumble polished, some of the better known being; petrified wood, agate and jade. Craftsmen in this field collect much of the material they use in the deserts, the mountains, and in many other locations. The other major souce for stones, especially those not available in local areas, is the rock shop or catalog supplier. There you will find rough and polished gemstones; supplies and tools; equipment for all kinds of gem cutting; mineral and crystal specimens; and a host of other intriguing items.

(3.) *Abrasive (grit).* Silicon carbide, a man-made abrasive in loose grain or powder form is used for grinding and smoothing the stones in a tumbler.

(4.) *A Polishing agent.* The final finish is most often accomplished with a polishing powder, usually an oxide of some metal. Grit and polishing agents are also sold by rock shops and catalog suppliers.

All of these items may be purchased separately, or some manufacturers do combine them in kit form. In addition to the equipment and materials listed above, these kits ususally include a supply of jewelry parts, a tube of jewelry cement and an instruction book. It's a convenient and inexpensive means for getting started in the craft.

There is a wide variety of gem materials available, many of which looks beautiful tumble polished. They come from three sources:

(1.) *Natural minerals formed in the earth*: A few examples of this category include agate, turquoise, garnet, petrified wood, and malachite; there are hundreds more.

(2.) *Products of aminal or plant life,* sucha s pearls, corral, amber or ivory.

(3.) *Man-made materials.* These include synthetics, which are laboratory duplicates of nature, such as synthetic rubies and sapphires.

Of the three categories above, the people who tumble gems use mostly material from the first — the natural stones.

Azurite from the Bagdad Mine

Azurite and malachite found in the copper country area

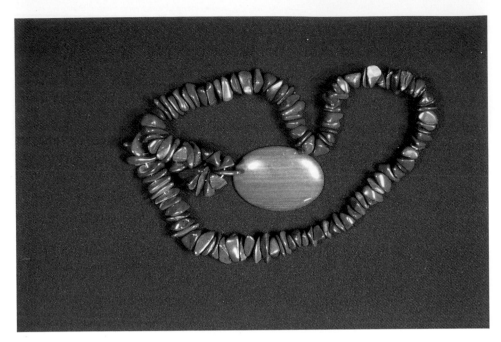

New River red jasper necklace

Red jasper found at Black Canyon

Peridot from the San Carlos area

Malachite and tourmaline

Globe onyx

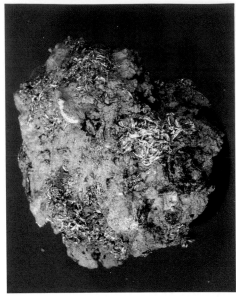

*Native silver collected in
southeast Arizona*

Turquoise

Arizona azurite, turquoise and malachite

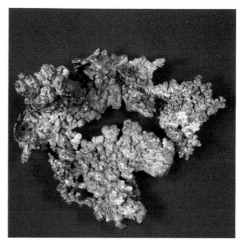

Top left: *Realgar and orpiment from Quartzsite*

Top right: *Natural copper*

Middle: *Porter Beds chalcedony roses*

Bottom left: *Pyrite cube from the Patagonia mining area*

Bottom right: *Wulfenite collected at the Red Cloud Mine area*

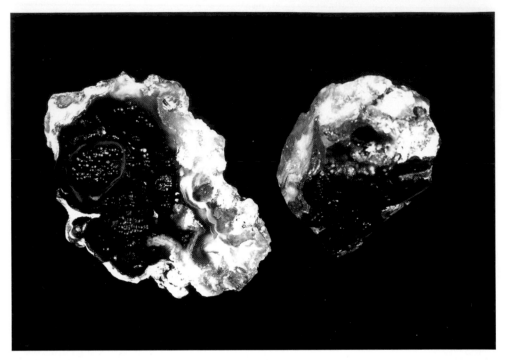

Fire agate collected along the Palo Verde gem trail

Chrysocolla on drusy quartz found near Superior

Quartz crystals

*Conglomerate from the
Mogollon Rim region*

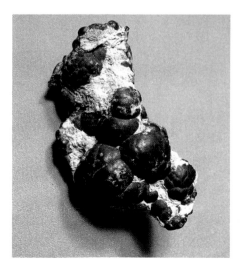

Bouse Hematite

*Pyrolusitic dendrites from the
Mogollon Rim*

Holbrook petrified wood

Agate and petrified wood

There are many other ways of classifying gemstones. One is the amount of light that can penetrate the material. Thus we have: transparent, semi-transparent, translucent and opaque. All are used for tumble polished gems, but you will probably see more opaque and translucent.

Another classification is by hardness, which in the mineral field is thought of as the ability of one stone to scratch another. This is quite important to the rockhound because generally (not always), the harder the gemstones, the more time required to work it , and the higher polish it will take. Also, the harder the stone, the longer it should retain its polish for there will be fewer substances in its environment that can scratch it.

Friedrich Mohs (1773-1839), a mineralogist, devised a scale for showing hardness with numerical designations of 1 for the softest through 10 for the hardest.

The Mohs Scale of Hardness

1 — Talc	6 — Feldspar
2 — Gypsum	7 —Quartz
3 — Calcite	8 — Topaz
4 — Flourite	9 — Corundum
5 —Apatite	10 — Diamond

It should be stated that these are relative hardnesses only. The Mohs Scale simply states that the stones listed will scratch any of those with lower numbers.

It is generally recommended that no material softer than glass be tumbled because they can be scratched easily, ruining the polish. In fact, it is a good idea not to use anything softer than quartz for items that can receive rough treatment — on a key chain, for instance. It is better to use softer stones for earrings, pendants, etc. Exceptions to this rule are the two types of jade, nephrite and jadeote. Although softer than quartz, they do not scratch easily.

For people who collect their own materials in the field, quite a few rock shops and catalog suppliers sell hardness testing kits. These consist of various minerals listed on the Mohs Scale. Inexpensive kits simply have samples of the minerals. On the better sets,pieces of the minerals are mounted in pencil-like handles for easier use.

Tumble polishing is man's improvement on a process that nature has been carrying out for ages. Tons of gemstones are tumbled commercially and sold at reasonable prices. But if you are a do-it-yourselfer, you can save money and have fun tumble polishing your own gems.

From *How to Tumble Polish Gemstones and Make Tumbled Jewelry* by Jerome Wexler

These two sites feature agate, jasper, and chalcedony, in a wide variety of colors and patterns. Most is found in shades of orange, red or green. Specimens containing all of those colors, together, are extremely nice when polished.

To get there, take Highway 60 three miles east from where it intersects Interstate 10. At that point, which is on the western edge of Brenda, turn north onto Perry Lane and go one and three-tenths miles. From there, proceed left and continue to the fork which is one and four-tenths miles farther. Site "A" is reached by continuing straight ahead, on the left branch, another seven-tenths of a mile.

From that point, and continuing at least one more mile, agate and jasper can be found in varying concentrations, on both sides of the road. Some of the material found at Site "A" is porous and thereby not capable of taking a good polish. It is essential to allow sufficient time to find the best that is available.

Site "B" is generally regarded as the more productive of the two, and is accessed by returning to the fork and, this time, bearing right seven-tenths of a mile. From there, and continuing at least another mile, one can pick up outstanding, bubbly chalcedony and lots of agate, some with interesting inclusions and delicate bands. There is also vividly colored jasper, in shades of red, yellow and gold, occasionally inundated with sharply contrasting black stringers. The road to Site "B" crosses a few sandy washes, and, for that reason, four-wheel drive might be needed. Don't attempt traveling places your vehicle is not intended to go.

This entire area is situated in open desert, and there are many suitable places to set up a camp. Supplies are available in nearby Quartzsite.

PLOMOSA MOUNTAINS

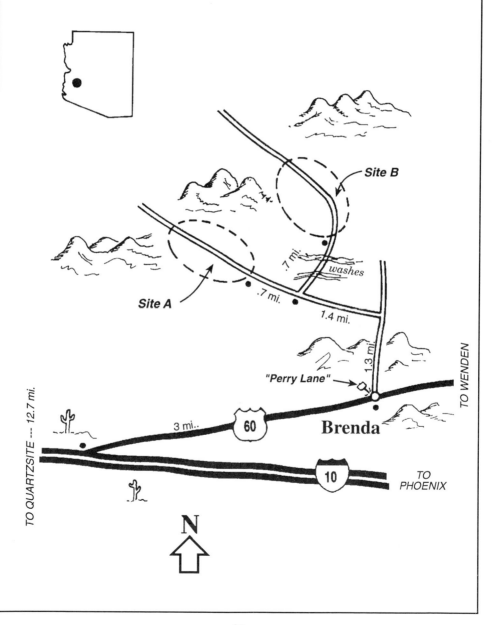

The low volcanic hills known as the Bear Hills, a short distance east of Brenda, contain a large amount of very colorful jasper. Specimens show a variety of markings and inclusions, including yellow and red flower patterns, moss, paisleys, and some streaked with purple and blue. In addition, there is a host of multicolored material, as well some possessing only single shades of yellow, orange, purple, or red. Pieces range from chips to sizable chunks.

To get to this easily accessible collecting site, go east four and one-half miles on Highway 60 from where it intersects Interstate 10. This is approximately one and one-half miles past what is left of Brenda and is the center of the collecting area. Be sure to pull well off the highway before stopping. There is a good place to do that about four-tenths of a mile farther east, and it is suggested you proceed to that spot for safety reasons.

Jasper is found throughout the hills on either side of the pavement, but primarily to the south. It is necessary to crawl under the highway fence to get to the mountain of jasper, but that isn't too difficult. Once past the fence, simply hike around the foothills and you should be able to pick up as much of the colorful cutting material as you want.

Looking for jasper south of the pavement

BRENDA JASPER

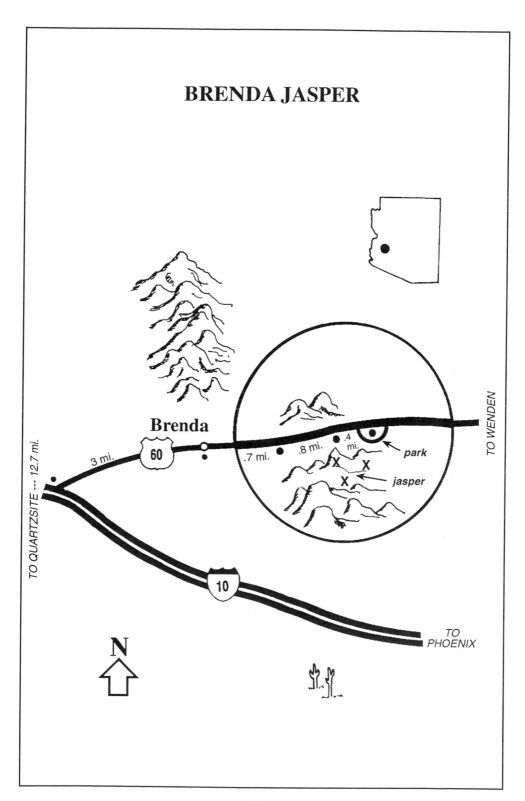

Quartz crystals, singles and clusters, can be obtained by following Eagle Eye Road north from Aguila as it climbs onto Indian Summit. The pavement ends after two miles and it gets very sandy at the three and nine-tenths miles point. Four-wheel drive will probably be necessary from time to time for the next two miles. After having gone six miles from the highway you will be at a gate. Be sure to close it after passing through, and continue along the road as it heads up the mountain.

At the summit, there is a three-way fork. Bear right, and go another nine-tenths of a mile. This section is rough, but most rugged vehicles should have no trouble. From there, proceed right again, and follow the tracks about two-thirds of a mile to the cliffs. Straight ahead is a dim trail going around the ridge to the crystal bearing quartz veins.

Crystals can occasionally be found lying on the ground below the veins, but the best are extracted from pockets and cavities in the host rock. This, of course, requires some tough labor with gads, chisels and sledge hammers in order to expose and remove the crystal bearing regions. Size varies from micromount to over two inches in length. Specimens range from perfectly clear to milky, with some exhibiting a faint pink hue.

There are a number of adequate places to camp at the summit, including the site parking area. Some of these upper regions offer spectacular views of the desert down below.

View of collecting area from below

AGUILA CRYSTALS

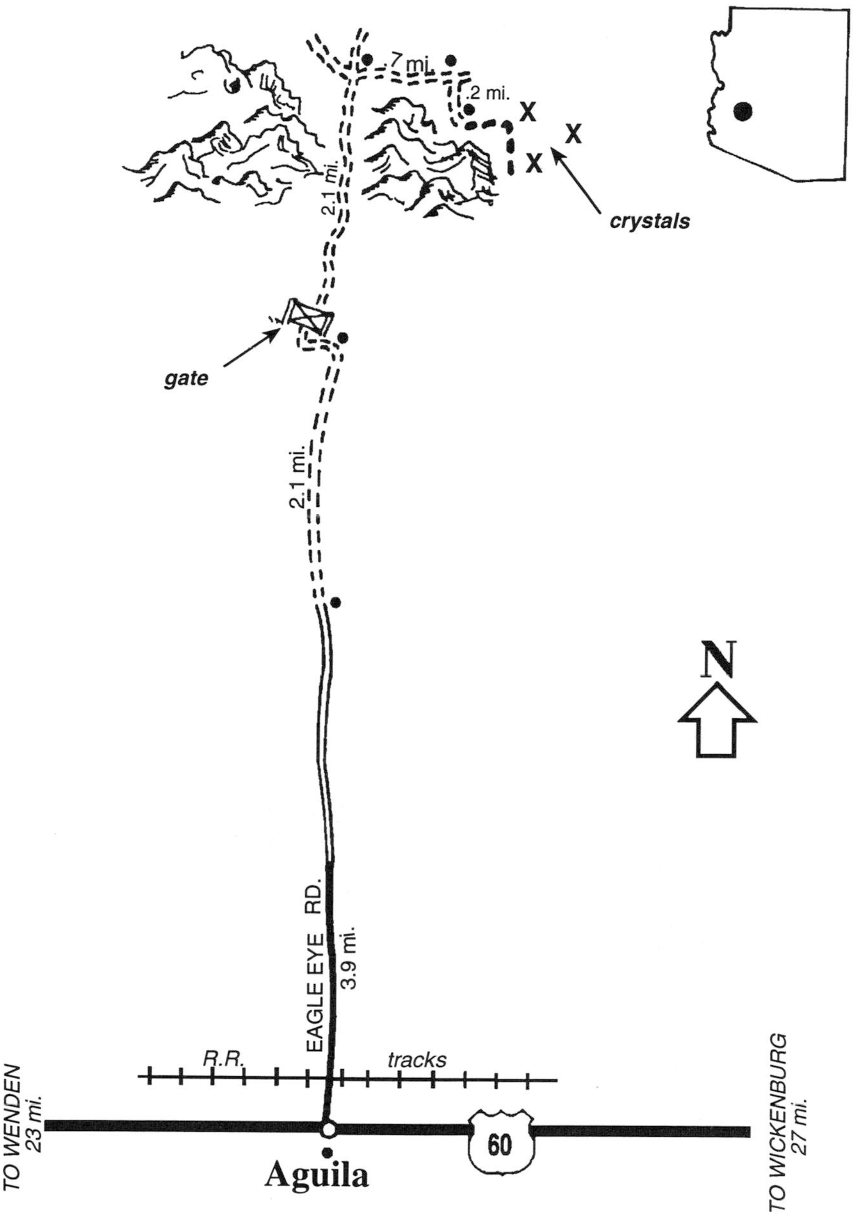

.7 mi.

.2 mi.

X

X

X

crystals

2.1 mi.

gate

2.1 mi.

N

EAGLE EYE RD.

3.9 mi.

R.R.   tracks

TO WENDEN
23 mi.

60

Aguila

TO WICKENBURG
27 mi.

Marble, in shades of pink, yellow and orange, with vivid contrasting bands and inclusions running throughout, can be obtained in the mountains southeast of Wenden. This material is generally solid enough to take a good polish and can be used to produce exquisite cabochons, spheres and bookends. Some contain crystal filled cavities, and such pieces, if encased in a colorful exterior, make beautiful display pieces, whether polished or left in their natural state.

To get to this very productive, but somewhat remote location, start one and eight-tenths miles east of Wenden on the dirt road heading south away from the black U.S. Manganese stockpile. Go through the gate, be sure to reclose it, and proceed along the pipeline road seven and three-tenths miles. At that point, turn left, doubling back toward the mountains one and one-tenth miles. From there the going gets rough. The roughness is caused by large chunks of marble all over the road and it might prove fruitful to stop and examine some of it. To get to the center of the collecting area, however, proceed one more mile to where the ridge meets the road.

Marble is scattered all over the surrounding terrain, having come from large seams in the mountain. Simply start exploring the area, trying to spot material with the best color and banding. Some pieces must be split, due to surface weathering, in order to properly discern the hidden interior quality.

Road leading past the marble deposit

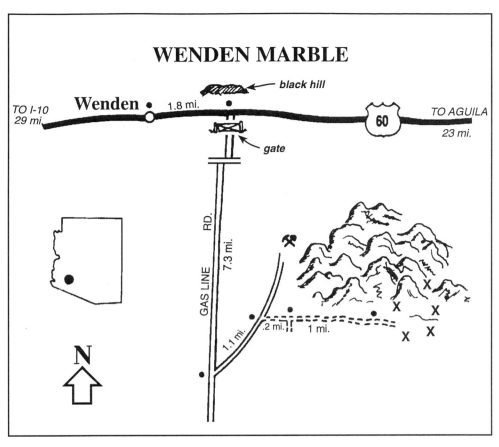

WENDEN MARBLE

black hill

Wenden • 1.8 mi.

TO I-10 29 mi.

TO AGUILA 23 mi.

60

gate

GAS LINE RD.

7.3 mi.

1.1 mi.

.2 mi.

1 mi.

N

A piece of Wenden marble

This site features botryoidal hematite, as well as colorful jasper, and it is not difficult to get to. Much of the hematite takes a nice polish, but well-formed botryoidal specimens are best left, as is, for display in a mineral collection. The jasper occurs in shades of yellow, orange and red, and it is also high quality.

To get to the center of this somewhat extensive collecting site from Bouse, go west on Plomosa Road, following the yellow center line, as it heads out of town. Proceed three and one-tenth miles to a cattle guard, and then, just three-tenths of a mile farther, a road will be seen heading off to the right. Follow that road one and three-tenths miles to the start of the collecting area. From there, continuing at least another mile west, you will find the hematite and jasper scattered randomly throughout the terrain.

It isn't too difficult to find lots of fine specimens by simply roaming the hillsides near the road. As is usually the case, it seems that the farther from the road you go, the larger the pieces become. The hematite is black or brown and thereby not tough to spot against the lighter colored soil. The largest specimens of either mineral can be obtained by digging in the seams situated in the foothills. This involves hard work, but the potential rewards help make it more bearable. Just look for signs of where others have been digging.

There are a few mining claims in the area, so be sure not to trespass onto any of them.

BOUSE HEMATITE & JASPER

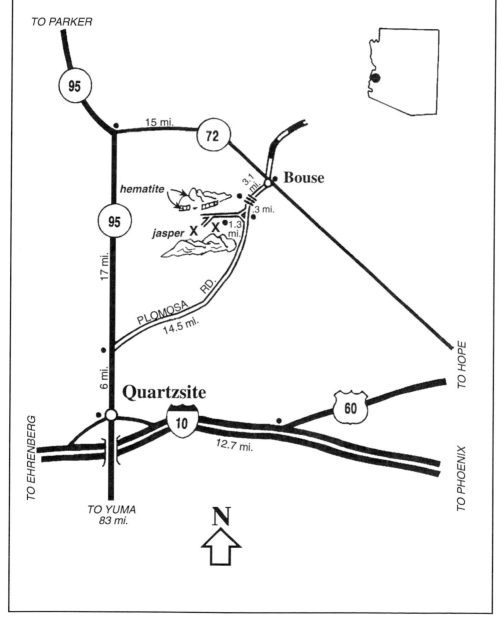

TO PARKER

95

15 mi.

72

Bouse

3.1 mi.

hematite

.3 mi.

95

jasper X X 1.3 mi.

17 mi.

PLOMOSA RD.

14.5 mi.

6 mi.

Quartzsite

10

60

12.7 mi.

TO HOPE

TO EHRENBERG

TO PHOENIX

TO YUMA
83 mi.

N

This remote site is not easy to get to and the trip should be attempted only in a four-wheel drive vehicle. The location boasts petrified wood and occasional chunks of colorful agate and jasper.

To get there from Quartzsite, go north from town one and eight-tenths miles either on Avenue 24E or Moon Mountain Road, and then jog to connect with the continuation of Moon Mountain Road, as shown on the map. Continue on this dirt road four and three-tenths miles to a fork. Stay to the right and continue an additional eighteen and two-tenths miles, bearing toward the distant cliffs in the northwest.

You will cross a number of washes along the way, but it is difficult to get off the main road. Just keep bearing to the northwest, following the sometimes dim tracks. At the proper mileage you will find yourself in yet another big wash, near the edge of some dirt hills. The wood is randomly scattered throughout those hills, along with occasional pieces of agate, jasper and jasp-agate.

It is recommended that you continue along the base of the hills another two and three-tenths miles to where the wash turns to the west. There, you can pull out of the sand and the hills are less steep.

Take some time to explore as much of this vast area as possible. The material close to the access road is not plentiful but an adequate amount can be picked up with a little patience.

Rockhounds can find limb sections, as well as delicate, perfectly formed twigs. The wood is primarily light brown and takes an excellent polish, often with orange streaks running throughout. The finest jasper is vivid red with white and blue stringers, and it is some of the most unusual I have ever found. It is scarce, but well worth looking for.

The dirt mounds at the collecting site

MOON MOUNTAIN PETRIFIED WOOD

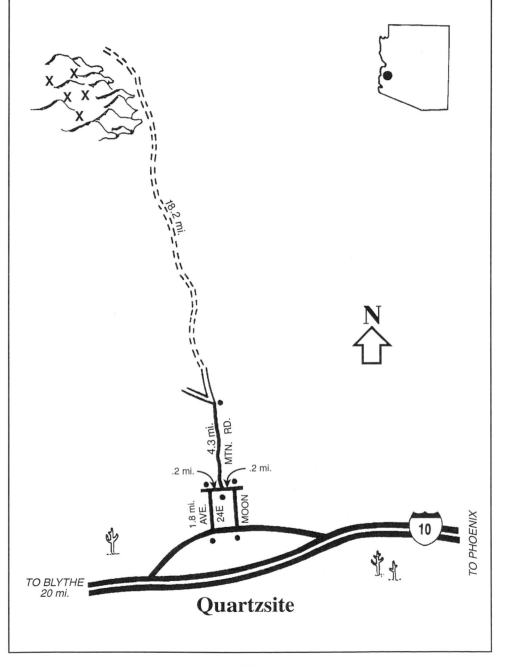

N

18.2 mi.

4.3 mi.

MTN. RD.

.2 mi.   .2 mi.

1.8 mi.

AVE.

24E

MOON

10

TO PHOENIX

TO BLYTHE
20 mi.

Quartzsite

These two sites provide collectors with a wide range of interesting minerals including onyx, quartz and ilmenite. To get there from Quartzsite, take the westernmost freeway overpass south to the frontage road and parallel the interstate three and nine-tenths miles to where you will spot some ruts heading into the hills. Follow those ruts six-tenths of a mile to the crossroad and then turn west another one-half mile. At that point, go south and continue four-tenths of a mile to Site "A" where you can find chert, as well as nicely patterned brown onyx, all over the hill. Both take a fairly good polish.

To get to Site "B", return to the frontage road and go west another eight-tenths of a mile, then turn south one and seven-tenths miles, driving around the hills, as shown on the map. You will be able to see the mine dumps on the hills, a few hundred yards away, those being a good source for fine specimens of ilmenite and other minerals. The metallic ilmenite frequently displays black platelike crystallization, and stands out beautifully against the exceptionally white host quartz. Such pieces make very nice additions to a mineral collection.

Since the status of mines change almost daily, be certain, when you visit, that collecting is not prohibited. If you have any concerns about the status of the mines, restrict yourself to washes and terrain below.

Road to Site "B"

QUARTZSITE MINERALS

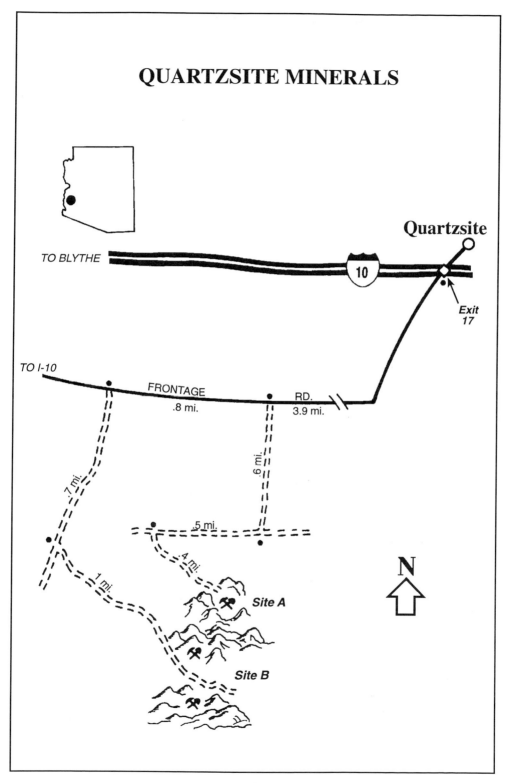

This location is one of Arizona's best known rockhounding sites and, as the name implies, it furnishes collectors with nice examples of perfectly formed quartz crystals. To get there, take Highway 95 south from Quartzsite nine miles to the BLM sign designating the turn to Crystal Hill. Follow that well graded dirt road six miles east to the campground, where you should park and commence your search. At the campground, there are restrooms and cleared campsites. There is no water, however, so you must bring your own, and, since this is hot arid desert country, water is a necessity!

The actual collecting is done in the wash to the north and on the hills opposite that wash. From below, you will be able to see where previous people have worked the quartz bearing seams. Those diggings form near perfect lines on the face of the cliffs, making them easy to spot.

There are two types of rockhounds who collect at Crystal Hill. The first is the ambitious hard rock collector who chips into the tough host rock, attempting to split the seams and free the beautiful crystals from their place in the mountain. That method involves hard work but the rewards are great if you discover a pocket. The other technique involves using a screen to sift through the loose soil on top of the hill, beneath the dumps, and in the wash below, hoping to discover crystals which have already been weathered free.

A few crystals contain natural inclusions, many of which can't be identified. Doubly terminated specimens are common. A few scepters have also been found here.

Parked at the base of Crystal Hill

CRYSTAL HILL

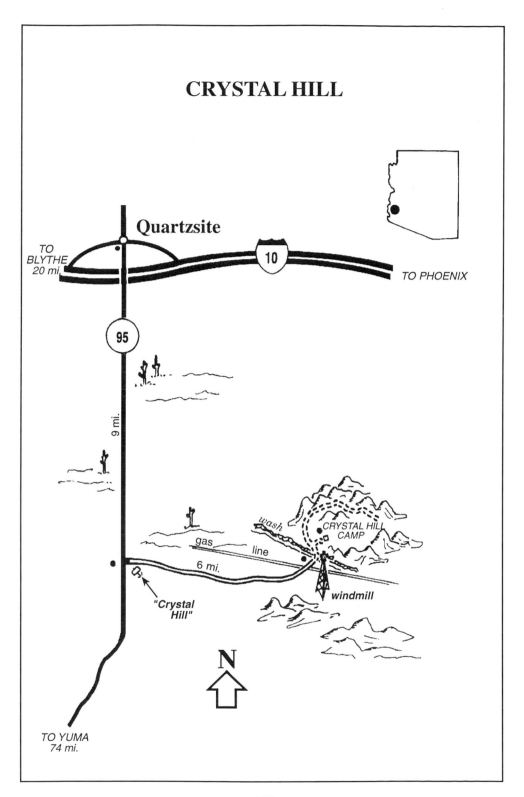

Quartzsite

TO BLYTHE 20 mi.

10

TO PHOENIX

95

9 mi.

wash

CRYSTAL HILL CAMP

gas line

6 mi.

windmill

"Crystal Hill"

N

TO YUMA 74 mi.

This is a fairly good location to pick up good solid chunks of colorful cutting material. To get there, go south nineteen miles from Quartzsite, on Highway 95, to the Palm Canyon turnoff. Turn east toward the mountains and follow the well-graded road about two miles to the start of the collecting area. From there, continuing at least another three miles, rockhounds can find agate, jasper, and even some nice chalcedony roses scattered randomly throughout the terrain. Be advised that this site is within the boundaries of the KOFA Wildlife Refuge, so you can only collect from the surface. No digging is allowed.

One of the difficulties with collecting here is that many of the rocks are covered with a dark desert varnish, thereby concealing their true identity. It is often necessary to split any suspect stone in order to accurately determine what it is. Frequently, that effort is rewarded with beautifully colored jasper, in shades of red, yellow and gold, or nice clear agate, sometimes filled with interesting inclusions.

It is suggested that you plan to do some walking away from the road in order to find the best this spot has to offer. Most of the easily accessible material near Palm Canyon Road has been picked up over the years, leaving only stones that have been recently unearthed or washed down from higher regions by the forces of erosion. Patience and determination are mandatory here, but the quality of what can be found often compensates for the inconvenience.

Looking for agate

PALM CANYON AGATE

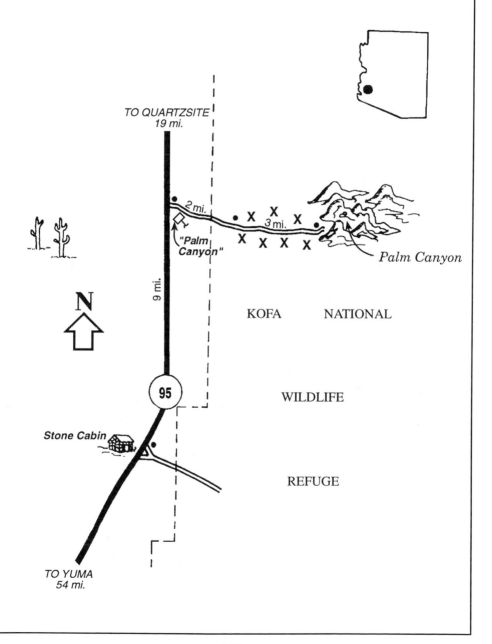

TO QUARTZSITE
19 mi.

2 mi.

X X X
3 mi. X
X X X X X

"Palm Canyon"

Palm Canyon

N

9 mi.

KOFA   NATIONAL

95

WILDLIFE

Stone Cabin

REFUGE

TO YUMA
54 mi.

This is a somewhat remote collecting site that offers rockhounds an opportunity to gather lots of well-formed chalcedony roses and some occasional chunks of agate. If you choose to make the journey, a rugged vehicle is necessary and it is a good idea to take extra supplies in case you are delayed.

To get there, proceed south from Quartzsite nine miles, on Highway 95, to the Crystal Hill turnoff. Follow that road six miles to Crystal Hill and then jog to the pipeline road, as shown on the map, continuing another twelve miles. At that point, park and explore the surrounding terrain.

Some of the best roses are found still encased within the tough host rhyolite where they were formed, and the best of those primary sources can be seen from where you park. Look south across the wash to the second escarpment on the ridge, that seems to be one of the most prolific spots. If you do trek to the ridge, it will be necessary to spend some time looking for roses that have been weathered far enough out so they can be removed without being damaged.

Roses can also be found randomly scattered throughout the flatlands for quite a distance in all directions. As shown on the map, this is an extensive area, so be sure to allow enough time for adequate exploration.

Some roses found here are colossal, often measuring many inches across. Another desirable attribute is that they all seem to fluoresce a bright greenish yellow, being welcome specimens for any collector with a fluorescent display.

Searching for roses on the way to the ridge

PORTER BEDS CHALCEDONY

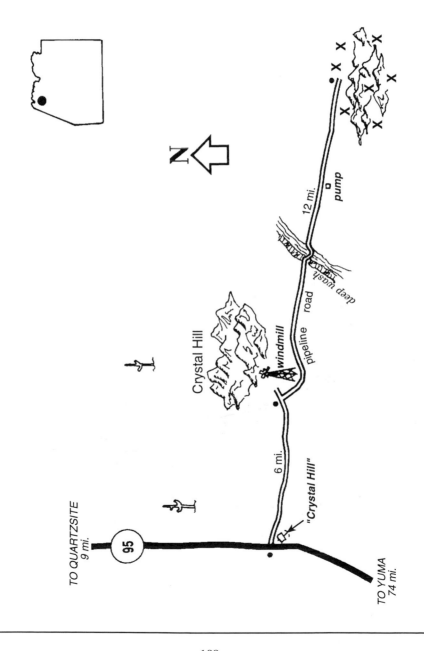

Copper minerals and fire agate can be found in the desert mountains about thirty-four miles east of Quartzsite. To get there from Interstate 10, take the Hovater Road Exit (Exit 53) and go south three-tenths of a mile, across the aqueduct, to the frontage road. From there, turn right, travel one-tenth of a mile and then turn left onto Harquahala Road, proceeding another eight-tenths of a mile. Just as the road starts to curve, ruts will be seen leading south to some mine dumps in the hills. Go as far as your vehicle can take you along those ruts and then hike the remaining distance to the old prospects.

A number of minerals can be found in the dumps including chrysocolla, malachite, pyrite, and bornite. The best specimens are obtained by doing some hard rock digging in the quartz seams, which involves difficult sledge hammer and chisel work. Occasionally, however, very good pieces can be found by just digging through the dumps. Take plenty of water if you plan to hike to the holes and watch for snakes.

A second potentially productive collecting site is situated on the opposite side of Interstate 10. To get there, cross over the highway, go north about six-tenths of a mile, and park. The region on and surrounding the little hill to the west contains lots of agate, some of which shows fire. This is a private claim held by the Quartzsite Gem and Mineral Society, and it may be necessary to pay their $3.00 annual membership dues in order to collect. Be sure to abide by any posted regulations, and, if you are unsure of the collecting status when you visit, don't collect there. You should still be able to find enough to keep you satisfied at the southern location.

Hiking the remaining distance to the old prospects

EAGLE TAIL MOUNTAINS

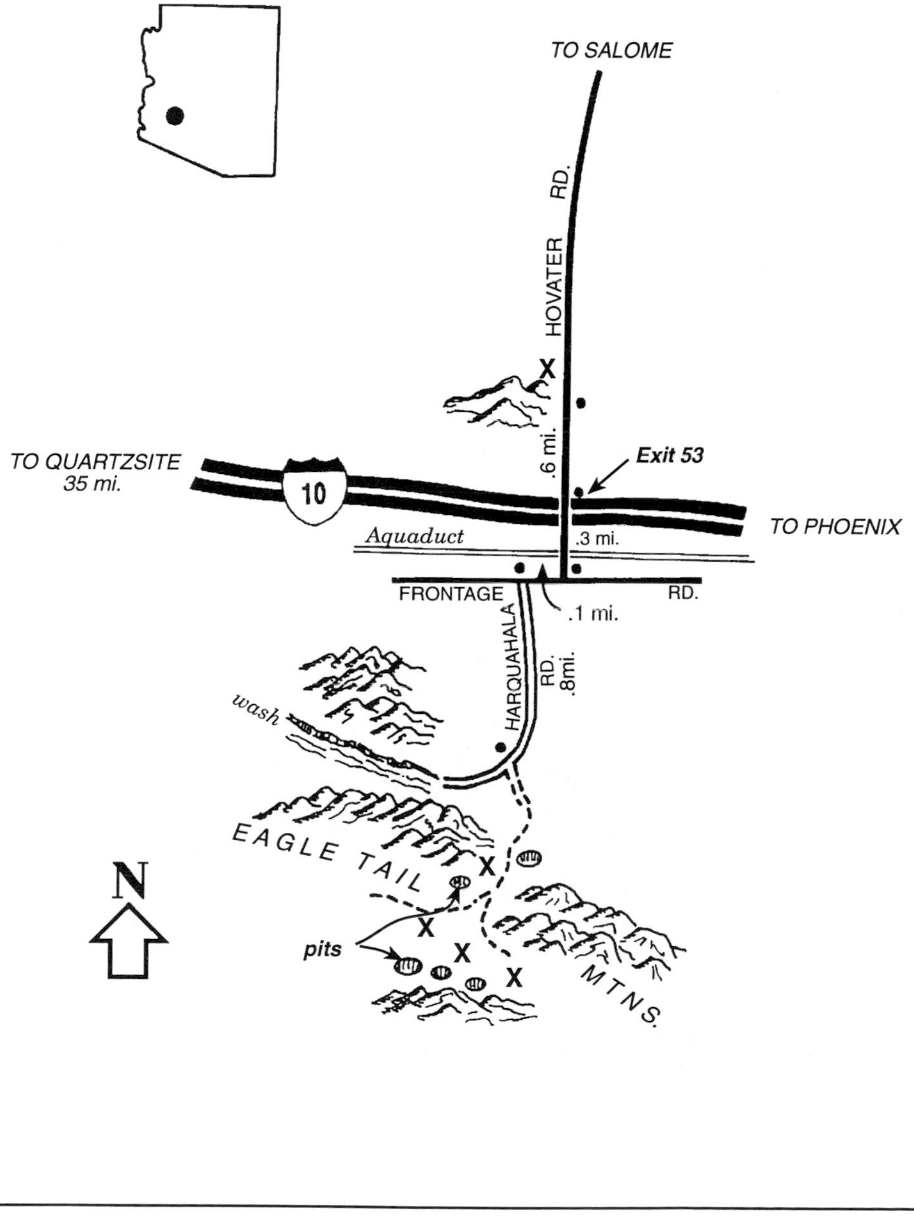

TO SALOME

HOVATER RD.

X

.6 mi.

TO QUARTZSITE
35 mi.

10

Exit 53

Aquaduct

.3 mi.

TO PHOENIX

FRONTAGE

RD.

.1 mi.

HARQUAHALA RD. .8mi.

wash

EAGLE TAIL

X

X

pits

X

X

X

MTNS.

N

The location shown on the map is situated in the KOFA National Wildlife Refuge, a shelter for bighorn sheep and other animals. No digging or use of hand tools is permitted within the refuge, so minerals can only be picked up loose from the surface. That does limit the quantity of what can be obtained here, but it seems that new material is washed from the hills just about every time it rains. Fire agate is not very plentiful, and it takes lots of patience and time to obtain even a few specimens, unless you are incredibly lucky.

To get to this scenic location, go south on Highway 95 from Quartzsite, about twenty-seven and one-half miles, to the ruins of Stone Cabin, as shown on the map. At that point, a road leads toward the mountains in the east, and that road should be followed another six and one-half miles to a fork. At the fork, bear right seven more miles and then turn west to the base of the mountains and start collecting.

Because this location is in the desert, it is not recommended for the summer months, and it is also essential that your vehicle be in good repair since it is somewhat remote.

Very fine chalcedony roses and occasional chunks of agate can be found throughout the desert flatlands, starting from where you leave Highway 95 and continuing into the foothills. A few of the roses contain tiny quartz crystals and can be used to make outstanding display pieces for a mineral collection.

Parked at the fire agate site

KOFA FIRE AGATES

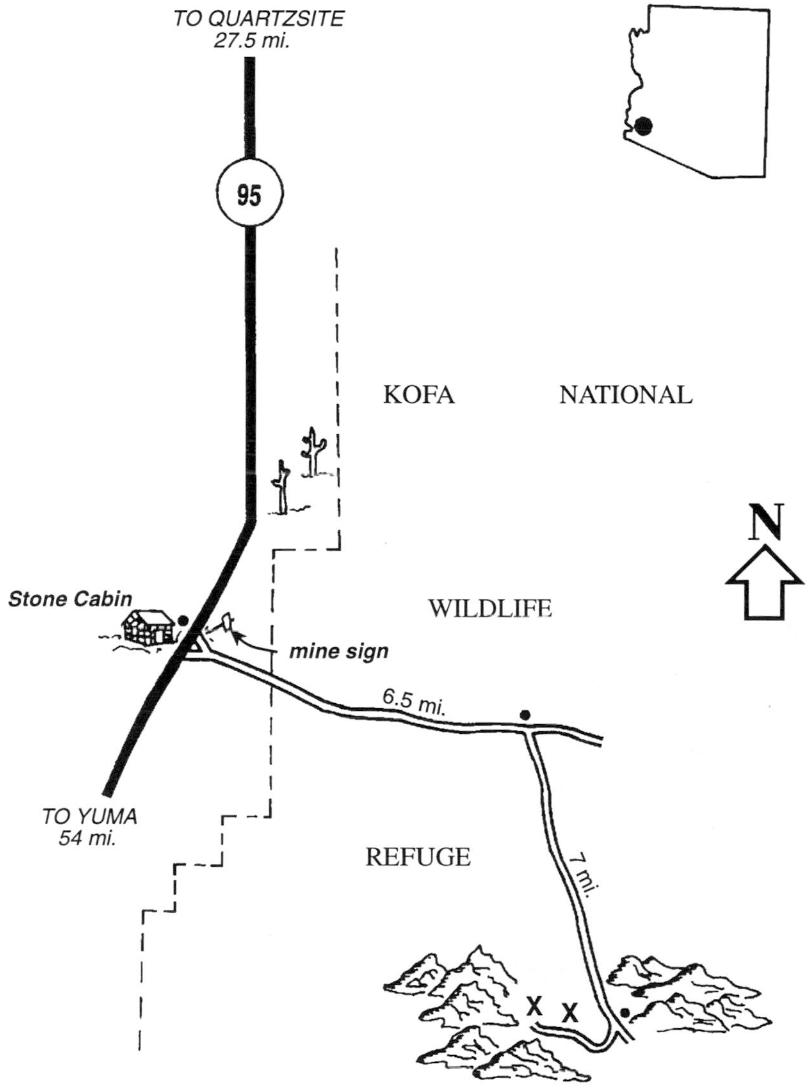

TO QUARTZSITE
27.5 mi.

95

KOFA   NATIONAL

N

Stone Cabin

mine sign

WILDLIFE

6.5 mi.

TO YUMA
54 mi.

REFUGE

7 mi.

X X

◆ — KOFA PASTELITE & ORBICULAR JASPER — ◆

These collecting areas provide an opportunity to obtain pastelite and or-bicular jasper, two interesting and somewhat uncommon materials. Site "A" is reached by going south from Quartzsite about nineteen miles on Highway 95 to the Palm Canyon turnoff and then continuing south another six and one-tenth miles to where tracks can be spotted leading east from the pavement toward the foothills. If you miss the turnoff, continue to Stone Cabin and then double back two and eight-tenths miles. Drive about one and one-half miles along those somewhat rough ruts to Site "A", at the base of the hills.

You will see the weathered remnants of where holes and trenches have been dug by previous rockhounds, which marks the primary deposit. The ma-terial found here is pastelite and it looks something like jasper, but doesn't have the glossy luster. Colors range from tan and pink to brown and red, with some specimens being quite sizable.

Site "B" is reached by returning to Highway 95 and going south another five and three-tenths miles. There, you must carefully pull off the pavement and explore the wash and surrounding regions east of the road for interesting orbicular jasper. This brown material is filled with fascinating round spots or "eyes", and can be used to make attractive cabochons, spheres and book ends.

It is found scattered throughout the area for quite a distance, or dug from seams on the side of the small hills. This location has been known for many years, and considerable collecting has been done, especially near the highway. It is suggested that you plan to hike toward the mountains, if you want to gather good quantities. Pay particularly close attention to the wash, which seems to be a consistent supplier of good material.

*A specimen of
orbicular jasper*

KOFA PASTELITE & ORBICULAR JASPER

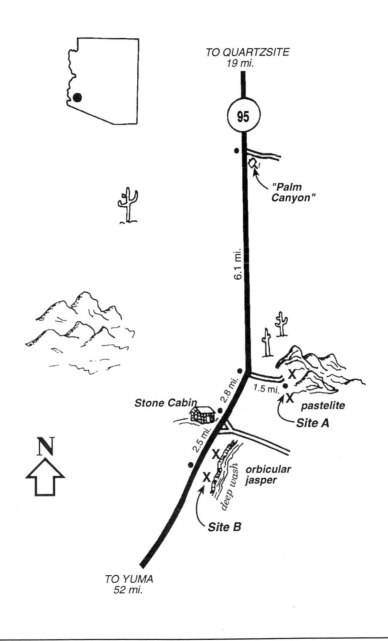

TO QUARTZSITE
19 mi.

95

"Palm Canyon"

6.1 mi.

2.8 mi.

1.5 mi.

Stone Cabin

X
X pastelite
Site A

N

2.5 mi.

X
X orbicular jasper
deep wash

Site B

TO YUMA
52 mi.

This site provides a variety of interesting minerals, including fluorite, vanadinite, calcite, anglesite, cerussite, petrified wood, and banded rhyolite. To get there, take Highway 95 approximately thirty-seven miles north from Yuma to milepost 55. At that point, there is a road leading east through the Yuma Proving Grounds to the KOFA Mountains. Follow that road about eight miles, abiding by all restrictions posted at the entrance.

From that point, and extending at least another three miles, the terrain is littered with mine dumps. It is on those dumps where fine specimens of cerussite, vanadinite, anglesite, calcite, and fluorite can be found. Be certain, however, that any mine you choose to explore is abandoned. At time of publication, some of those once deserted dumps were being reactivated. Do not trespass onto any active mining claim and be certain to stay out of all shafts.

In addition to the mines, the flatlands throughout this region are littered with often colorful rhyolite and occasional chunks of brown petrified wood. Take some time to search for those minerals, also, since they can be used to produce nice polished pieces. Much of that material is covered with a dark desert varnish. Splitting may be necessary to properly discern what is otherwise concealed beneath the black exterior. Collecting in the KOFA National Wildlife Refuge is restricted to surface gathering only. Do not do any digging.

Gathering specimens at the collecting site

CASTLE DOME AREA MINERALS

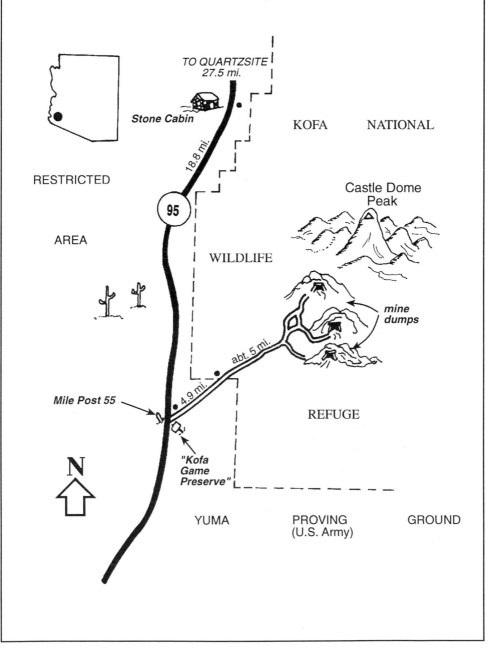

TO QUARTZSITE
27.5 mi.

Stone Cabin

KOFA   NATIONAL

RESTRICTED

18.8 mi.

95

Castle Dome
Peak

AREA

WILDLIFE

mine
dumps

abt. 5 mi.

Mile Post 55

4.9 mi.

REFUGE

N

"Kofa
Game
Preserve"

YUMA   PROVING   GROUND
              (U.S. Army)

Apache tears can be found throughout the desert flatlands southeast of Aguila, at the location designated as Site "A" on the accompanying map. To get there, go south out of town five miles and then bear left at the fork another seven miles. The center of the collecting area is situated just after passing through a big wash, and the tears can be found randomly scattered on both sides of the road for quite a distance.

The exterior surface of these Apache tears is sometimes deceiving, since they can be somewhat dull and opaque. Don't let that fool you. After polishing, most will indeed be transparent, with many displaying interesting bands or a silken sheen, which, when polished, produces spectacular cat's-eyes. In addition to the tears, collectors can gather brilliant white chalcedony, some of it banded and capable of producing great cabochons.

Drive three and seven-tenths miles farther east and there will be a small quarry on the north side of road, which is Site "B". In and around that old mine, rockhounds can find chalcedony and little crystal filled, geode-like bubbles of limestone. These fascinating little orbs frequently make great display pieces in a mineral collection.

Be sure, while in the area, to continue to the old Vulture gold mine. This once rich prospect was discovered in 1863 and proved to be one of Arizona's most productive mines. It is now inactive and being run as a museum. The small admission fee is well worth it if you have time to stop.

Polished Apache tears

VULTURE MINE REGION

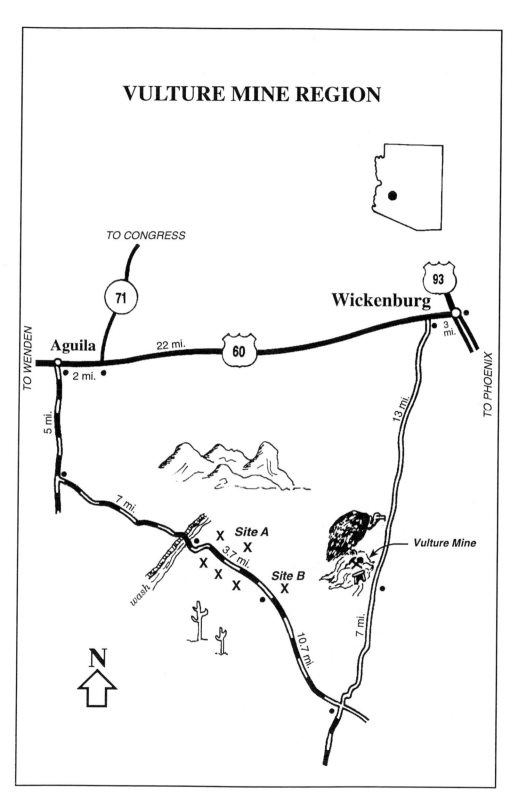

TO CONGRESS

71

93

Wickenburg

TO WENDEN

Aguila 22 mi. 60

3 mi.

TO PHOENIX

2 mi.

5 mi.

13 mi.

7 mi.

Site A

X X
X
3.7 mi.
X X Site B
X X X X Vulture Mine

wash

10.7 mi.

7 mi.

N

To get to the agate location, take Interstate 8 approximately five miles west from Gila Bend to the Painted Rocks turnoff, and head north ten and six-tenths miles. The mountains will be on your right and dim tracks lead off to the northeast. Follow those tracks a short distance and you should be able to spot pieces of agate and occasional, small quartz crystals randomly scattered about. From there, hunt toward the mountains.

If you do not feel your vehicle is capable of traveling on the old road, park well off the pavement and hike. The agate is not extremely plentiful, but the colors and internal inclusions make the search worthwhile.

The old Rowley lead mine is located approximately one and one-half miles farther down the road, toward Painted Rocks Dam. The Rowley is known throughout the world as a classic locality for beautiful wulfenite specimens. Not only is this a good place to find wulfenite, but you can also collect mimetite, cerussite and chrysocolla. Be advised that this is considered to be a very dangerous mine, so be cautious, observe all warning signs and do not enter any shafts or tunnels! It is essential that you restrict your collecting to surface areas. Digging through the dumps and carefully breaking up suspect stones and boulders is probably the most efficient way to collect here.

If you have time, be sure to visit Painted Rocks State Park, about three more miles along the road. There, you can see a small rocky mountain covered with ancient graffiti. It is fun to try to figure out what the symbols might mean and why they were etched there in the first place.

Painted Rocks State Park

PAINTED ROCKS AGATE & MINERALS

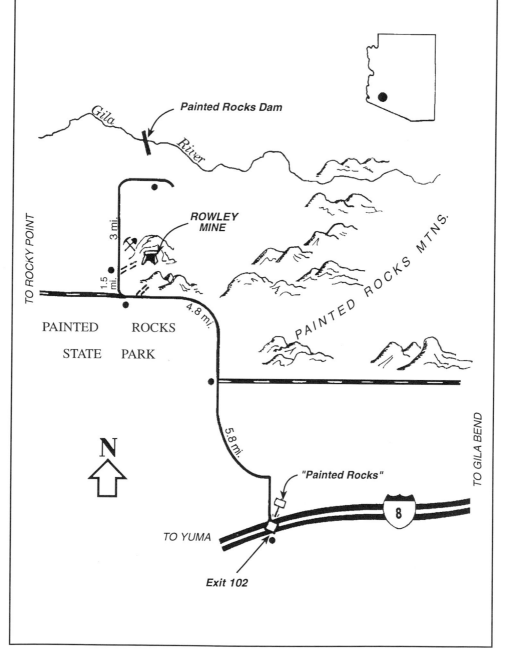

Painted Rocks Dam

Gila River

ROWLEY MINE

PAINTED ROCKS MTNS.

TO ROCKY POINT

3 mi.

1.5 mi.

4.8 mi.

PAINTED ROCKS

STATE PARK

N

5.8 mi.

TO GILA BEND

"Painted Rocks"

8

TO YUMA

Exit 102

The beautiful banded agate found near Fourth of July Peak, north of Gila Bend, is well known among southwest rockhounds. To get there, take the Hassayampa Road north from town about thirty miles to Agua Caliente Road. The turnoff is well marked and opposite some large cattle pens, making it fairly easy to spot. From there, go west one and one-tenth miles and then bear right, off the pavement. Follow that well-graded road fourteen and three-tenths miles and turn onto the tracks heading off to the right. Continue about six-tenths of a mile to the old chimney, which marks the center of Site "A", locally known as the Chimney Beds. From there, all the way to Fourth of July Peak, six miles farther west, agate can be found, in varying concentrations.

The agate is obtained by simply walking in any direction and keeping an eye out for the telltale little white stones. Most has a white opaque exterior and can be found on the flatlands, as well as in washes or other areas of erosion. Interiors tend to be light gray, with very delicate, fine, concentric white bands. One can also procure red, blue and gray moss agate, but it isn't plentiful and takes some patient searching to find. Most of what can be picked up from the surface is small. It is sometimes possible to get larger pieces by digging.

At Fourth of July Peak, Site "B", rockhounds can obtain more of the banded agate, multicolored agate, crystals, and even some Apache tears. As before, just roam through the surrounding countryside to find specimens.

The old chimney marking the center of Site "B"

FOURTH OF JULY PEAK AGATE

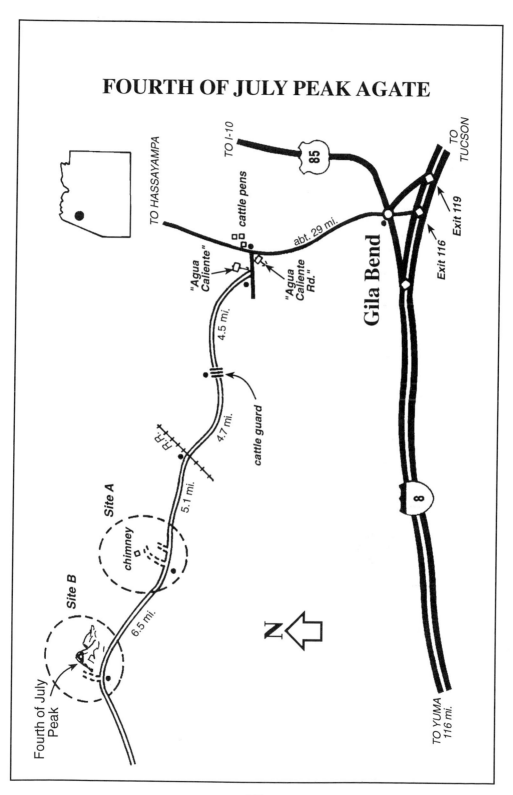

Saddle Mountain has been an eminent southwest mineral collecting spot for many years, primarily due to the beautiful fire agate and chalcedony that can be found there. In addition, rockhounds can occasionally find crystal-filled geodes on the lower slopes, but they are not too common.

To get there, go about seventy-five miles east of Quartzsite, on Interstate 10, to the Tonopah offramp (Exit 94), and head south two and seven-tenths miles. From there, turn right onto the Salome Highway, continue five and one-tenth miles, turn left, and proceed six-tenths of a mile farther to where some ruts will be seen heading toward the mountains on the south. Take any of them about one-half mile to the base of prominent Saddle Mountain.

From wherever you park in the lower slopes, the ground will be littered with chalcedony, all the way back to the pavement. Some of that chalcedony contains telltale brown and orange regions which indicate the potential of containing precious fire. Any pieces with such dark regions should be examined carefully and, possibly even dipped in water, to more accurately determine if they posses the beautiful, color-filled fire.

Most of the prime fire agate deposits were located high on Saddle Mountain and have been completely worked out. There are, however, numerous chalcedony seams running throughout the mountain and some could contain fire, further in. If you feel like doing some hard rock work with gads, chisels and sledge hammers, you might want to try your luck at working those areas.

Parked at the base of Saddle Mountain

SADDLE MOUNTAIN FIRE AGATE

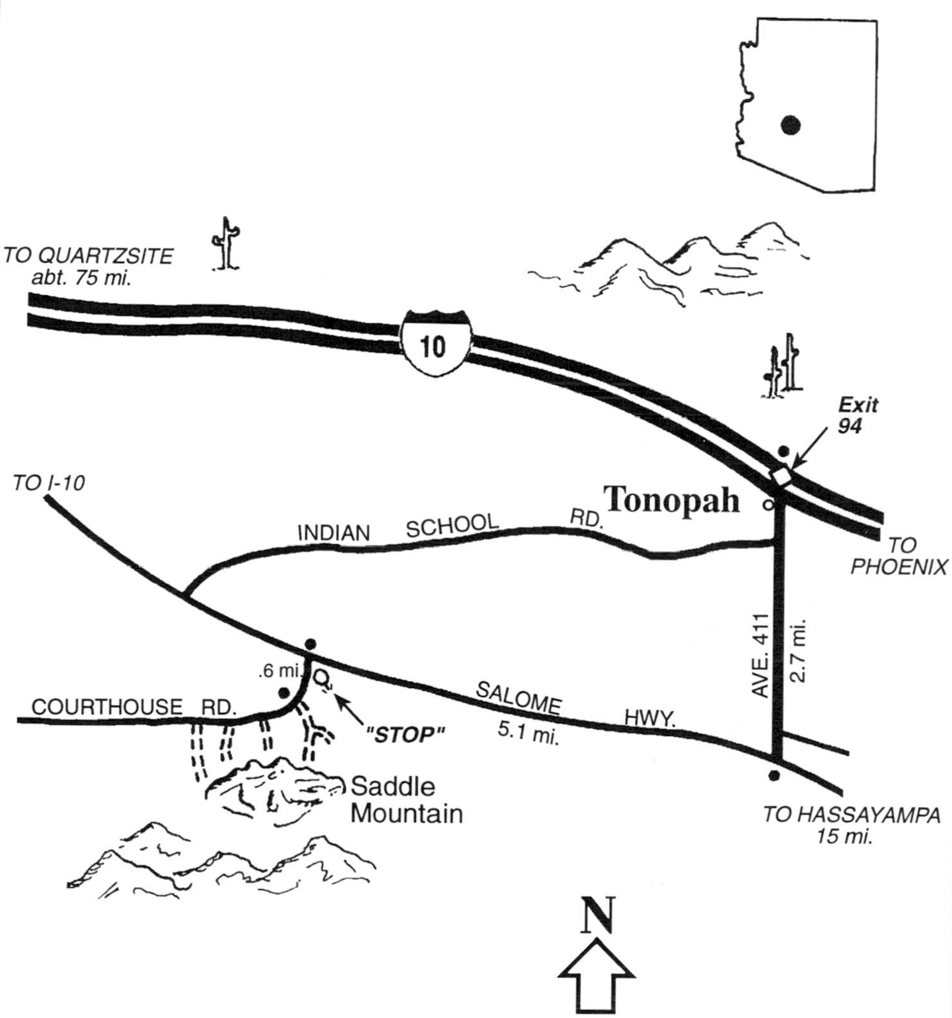

TO QUARTZSITE
abt. 75 mi.

10

TO I-10

Exit
94

Tonopah

INDIAN   SCHOOL   RD.

TO
PHOENIX

AVE. 411

2.7 mi.

.6 mi.

COURTHOUSE   RD.

SALOME   HWY.
5.1 mi.

"STOP"

Saddle
Mountain

TO HASSAYAMPA
15 mi.

N

The remnants of three old mining towns, Stanton, Octave and Weaver, offer mineral collectors a most interesting place to gather nice specimens. To get there, travel north two miles from Congress Junction, on Highway 89, to where there is a well-marked, graded dirt road heading east. Follow that road approximately four and one-half miles to a large wash.

Within that wash, in either direction, one can pick up nice mineral specimens. Due to erosion, however, the surfaces of most stones are quite abraded, thereby concealing their true identities. Any suspect rock should be spit to better determine what treasures might be otherwise hidden inside. The wash contains, among other things, stones containing tourmaline and pyrite, as well as colorful jasper.

Continue another mile and one-half to the remnants of Stanton. All along this road, and throughout most of the terrain of the immediate area, there is lots of collecting potential. Be sure to stop, from time to time, in order to do a good job of sampling.

The ownership status of Stanton, a once thriving little town, is continually changing, and you should not explore the site unless granted permission to do so. Gold was the reason for Stanton's existence and there is still some mining being done in the vicinity, all the way north to Yarnell and east to the ghost towns of Octave and Weaver. Little remains of Octave and Weaver, except a few overgrown foundations. A metal detector might be fun to use in hopes of discovering a few interesting artifacts from the past.

Be sure to search any wash in this area, as well as any abandoned mine dump. The jasper and occasional agate can be found randomly scattered throughout the region, and the dumps and some washes also provide good clean quartz, epidote, tourmaline, pyrite, hematite, fluorite, garnet, and gold. This is a fascinating region, full of history. Even if you don't find spectacular specimens, a journey through this part of Arizona should be well worth the time.

GHOST TOWNS & MINERALS

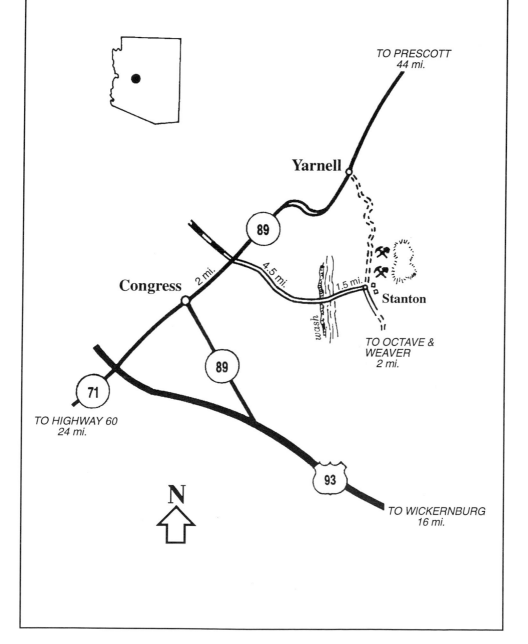

TO PRESCOTT
44 mi.

Yarnell

89

Congress   2 mi.   4.5 mi.

1.5 mi.   Stanton

wash

TO OCTAVE &
WEAVER
2 mi.

89

71

TO HIGHWAY 60
24 mi.

93

N

TO WICKERNBURG
16 mi.

There are only a few places where top quality dumortierite can be found, and one of those is just west of the state line, near Winterhaven, California. Dumortierite is an aluminum ore, varying in shades from an extremely bright, vivid blue to almost purple. In addition to dumortierite, the locality also offers good quantities of top quality agate and other minerals.

To get to there, take Interstate 8 to the Ogilby Road turnoff, which is about fifteen miles west of Yuma. Travel north thirteen and six-tenths miles and then turn east onto Indian Pass Road. From there, go an additional seven and three-tenths miles to the western edge of this fairly widespread rockhounding area.

The dumortierite is easy to spot, since most is bright blue. Simply walk a distance through the hills and washes when conducting your search. Material can be found in a wide range of qualities, so try to obtain only the best the location has to offer.

This site is primarily known for dumortierite, but also be on the lookout for agate and petrified palm. The agate sometimes contains fascinating inclusions and occurs in a wide range of colors. There is also some bright green epidote strewn about and some excellent mica specimens, often in combination with blue kyanite crystals. The latter, however, is somewhat rare.

Searching for dumortierite at the collecting area

INDIAN PASS DUMORTIERITE

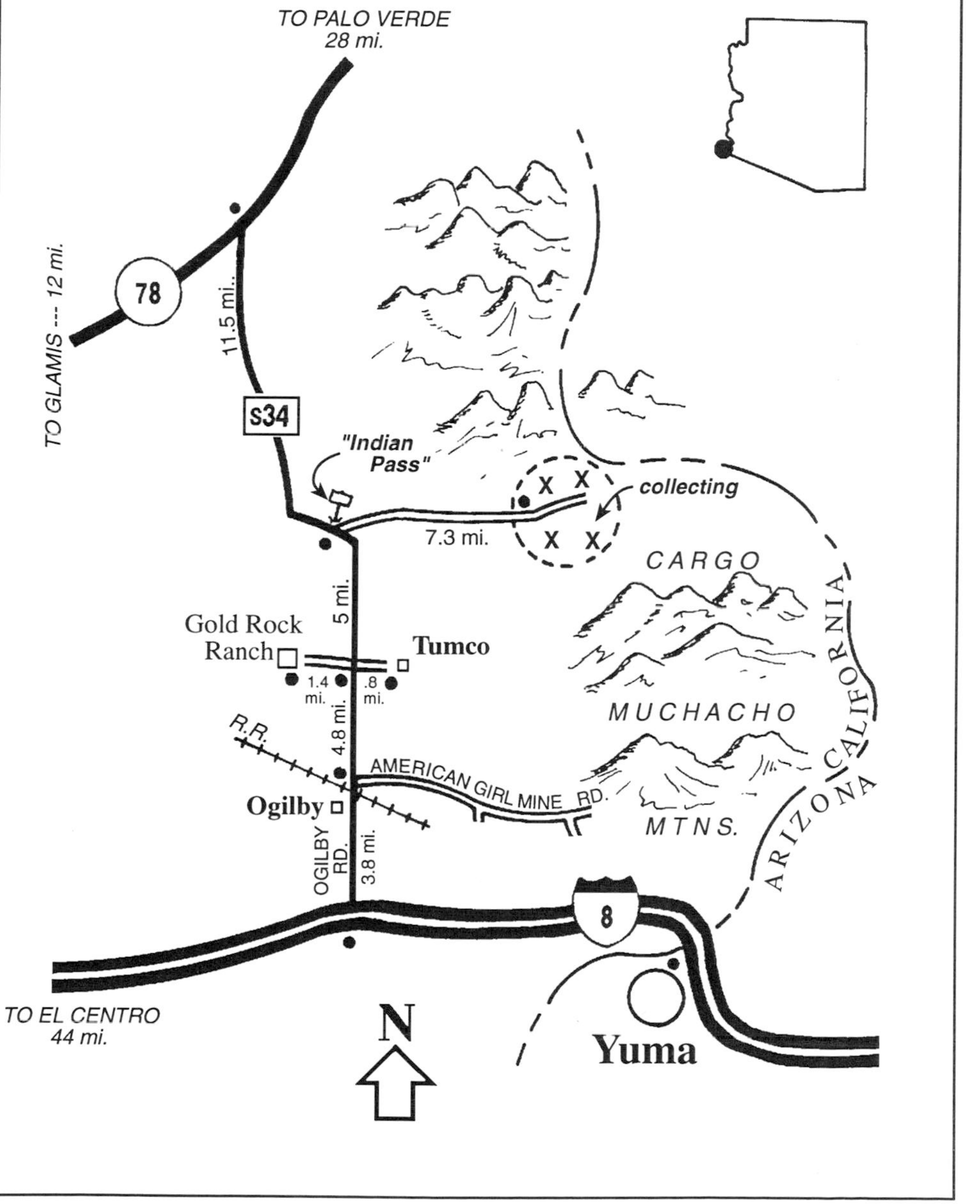

TO PALO VERDE
28 mi.

TO GLAMIS --- 12 mi.

78

11.5 mi.

S34

"Indian Pass"

X X   collecting
7.3 mi.
X X

CARGO

5 mi.

Gold Rock Ranch

Tumco

1.4 mi. .8 mi.

MUCHACHO

R.R.

4.8 mi.

AMERICAN GIRL MINE RD.

Ogilby

MTNS.

OGILBY RD.

3.8 mi.

ARIZONA

CALIFORNIA

8

TO EL CENTRO
44 mi.

N

Yuma

This is a fee location situated just west of the Arizona/California border. This site is probably one of the best places to collect fire agate anywhere in the country, unless you own your own claim. As an added bonus, there is also lots of nice chalcedony, agate, tiny quartz crystals, apatite, barite, calcite, clinoptilolite, fluorite, curved gypsum, and, just across the road, some nice geodes.

To get to the Opal Hill Fire Agate Mine, go west from Highway 78 on Fourth Street, at the southern edge of Palo Verde, as shown on the map. At the one mile mark, it will appear as if you are in someone's front yard, but the road goes around the house and heads through the sand hills toward the mountains. Follow the main road as it crosses Pebble Terrace, transits a couple of washes, and then heads into the mountains. Total distance from town is just under nine miles. The left-hand turn to the mine office can easily be seen at the given mileage.

At time of publication, the fee was $15 per person per day, but there are weekly, senior citizen, and group rates also available. The fee is a real bargain when you consider the value of what most people are able to find here. It isn't easy to remove the fiery gemstones from their place in the tough host rock. The mine owners, Nancy Hill and her husband Howard Fisher, are very helpful, and will make sure you get the most from your efforts. Be certain to take a good rock hammer, chisel, whisk broom, gloves, goggles, and a long handled screw driver, as a minimum tool supply, and be ready to do some tough work. In addition, take lots to drink, since working in this arid climate can make you very thirsty, and the nearest supplies are nine rough miles away, in Palo Verde.

The geodes are found in a number of locations in and immediately surrounding the Opal Hill Mine, most notably, a new deposit recently discovered just across the canyon. Nancy or Howard will direct you to those locations when you are there. If you want to dig for the geodes, you will need a pick, shovel, hand trowel, and other such equipment.

Camping is available at the mine, for a fee of $5 per night. They are open from November 1st until May 1st, and further information can be obtained by writing to Nancy Hill, Opal Hill Mine, P.O. Box 497, Palo Verde, CA 92666.

PALO VERDE FIRE AGATE

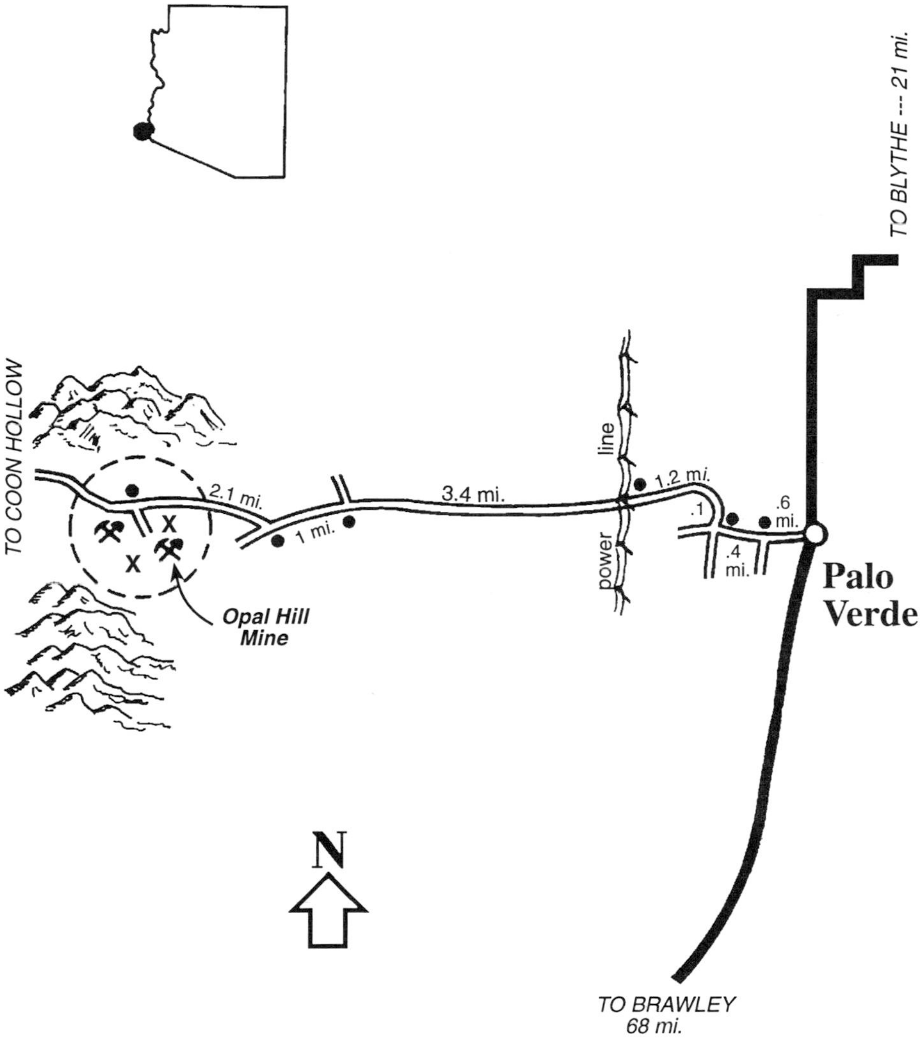

TO BLYTHE --- 21 mi.

TO COON HOLLOW

2.1 mi.

3.4 mi.

1 mi.

power line

1.2 mi.

.1

.6 mi.

.4 mi.

Opal Hill Mine

Palo Verde

TO BRAWLEY
68 mi.

N

One of Arizona's most notable mining areas is situated along the eastern edge of the Colorado River, just north of Imperial Dam. It is known as the Red Cloud District, and was made famous by the brilliant red-orange wulfenite crystals that have been found there.

Collecting status at the Red Cloud, as well as at any of the other numerous nearby mines, continually changes. At time of publication, rockhounds were allowed onto the Red Cloud dumps, for a small fee. Other nearby and less notable prospects are generally abandoned and open to surface collecting. That can change, making it essential that you accurately determine the status of any dump you choose to explore. On the map, are listed a few of the more productive mines, and a partial list of what can be obtained includes calcite, quartz, cerussite, smithsonite, galena, goethite, barite, vanadinite, fluorite, and, of course, wulfenite.

The caretaker at the Red Cloud Mine is very helpful in assisting rockhounds and providing up to date collecting information about other local dumps. For that reason, it is suggested that you make the Red Cloud your first stop. The road all the way to the Papago, Black Rock, and Red Cloud mines is generally in good condition and most rugged vehicles should have no trouble getting that far, but four-wheel drive might be needed to cross the big sandy wash. The route from the Red Cloud to the Dives, Princess, and Padre King is very rough, however, and four-wheel drive then becomes a necessity.

It has been reported that many of the local washes contain gold, so, if you have time and some dry washing equipment, it might be worth trying your luck.

En route to the mines, you must cross the Yuma Proving Ground. Be certain to read the sign posted near Highway 95 and, if a red flag is flying, do not enter! The flag indicates that they are doing some live bombing.

RED CLOUD MINE AREA

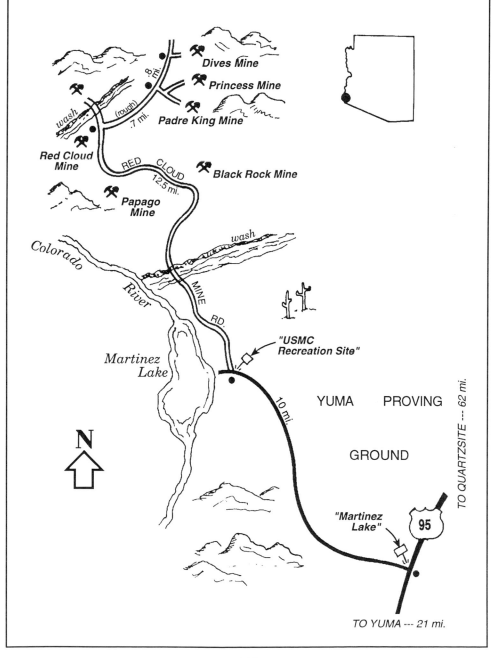

Dives Mine

Princess Mine

.8 mi.

(rough)

.7 mi.

Padre King Mine

wash

Red Cloud Mine

RED CLOUD 12.5 mi.

Black Rock Mine

Papago Mine

Colorado River

wash

MINE RD.

"USMC Recreation Site"

Martinez Lake

10 mi.

YUMA   PROVING

GROUND

N

TO QUARTZSITE --- 62 mi.

"Martinez Lake"

95

TO YUMA --- 21 mi.

This is where the prized Whipple Mountain pink chalcedony roses are found. These highly regarded roses can be used to produce exquisite cabochons or, in many cases, left as is for display in a mineral collection. The site is actually in California, but only a few miles west of the border.

To get there from Parker, go west on Highway 62 about seventeen miles to Vidal Junction and turn north onto Highway 95. Proceed another nine and seven-tenths miles to the large wash where some tracks will be seen, just north of that wash, leading toward the mountains. Follow the ruts a far as you can, stopping a few times along the way. The road is rough in places and goes through some loose sand. Four-wheel drive is desirable if you want to make it all the way to the mountains.

Generally, the chalcedony can be found just about anywhere from Highway 95 extending east all the way to the foothills, about five and one-half miles away. It is unusual, but some places are virtually void of the chalcedony, while, only a short distance farther, the desert pavement might be loaded with it. The bright white and pink color makes it very easy to spot against the darker soil and it doesn't take long to gather quite a few pieces.

Remember that this is an arid and desolate region. Take extra water. If you choose to hike away from the highway, do not lose your bearings or go so far that it might be difficult or impossible to get back.

WHIPPLE MOUNTAIN CHALCEDONY

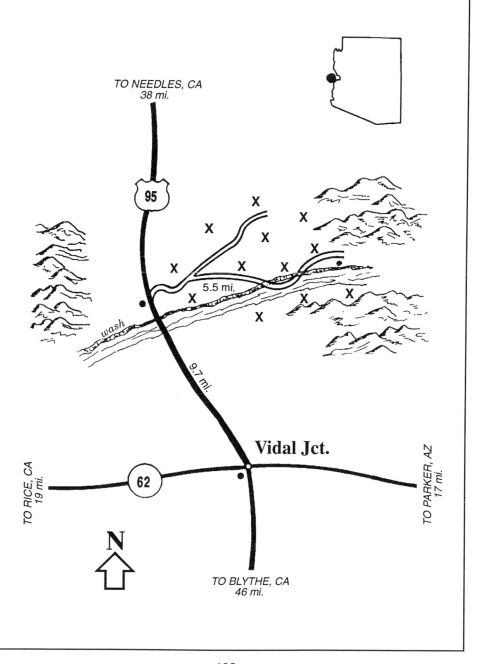

TO NEEDLES, CA
38 mi.

95

X X X X X X

5.5 mi.

X X X X X

wash

X X

9.7 mi.

Vidal Jct.

TO RICE, CA
19 mi.

62

TO PARKER, AZ
17 mi.

N

TO BLYTHE, CA
46 mi.

Red, yellow, green and brown jasper can be found here, as well as chunks of colorful jasp-agate, banded agate and chert. The location is actually in California, but only a short distance west of the border.

To get to the center of the collecting area from the tiny town of Earp, which is on the opposite side of the Colorado River from Parker, head west on Highway 62 three and eight-tenths miles. At that point, there will be a turn to the south toward Big River. The road leading to the collecting area is only three-tenths of a mile farther west. The turnoff is difficult to spot from the pavement and is just beyond where the power lines cross the highway. Turn to the right off the road, at the power lines. As you rise from the pavement, the ruts can be spotted, a few yards away, heading north toward the mountains. Follow those ruts one and three-tenths miles to the edge of the agate and jasper field.

Material can be found for quite a distance scattered throughout the surrounding hills, on both sides of the road. If you allow enough time, and are willing to do some walking, this location could provide a considerable quantity of outstanding cutting material.

Some of the specimens are covered with a dark desert varnish, so you will have to carefully scrutinize each piece in order to determine its true nature. Often, splitting suspect stones will reveal the quality of what might be hidden inside.

Examining a rock covered in desert varnish to determine its true nature

BIG RIVER AGATE

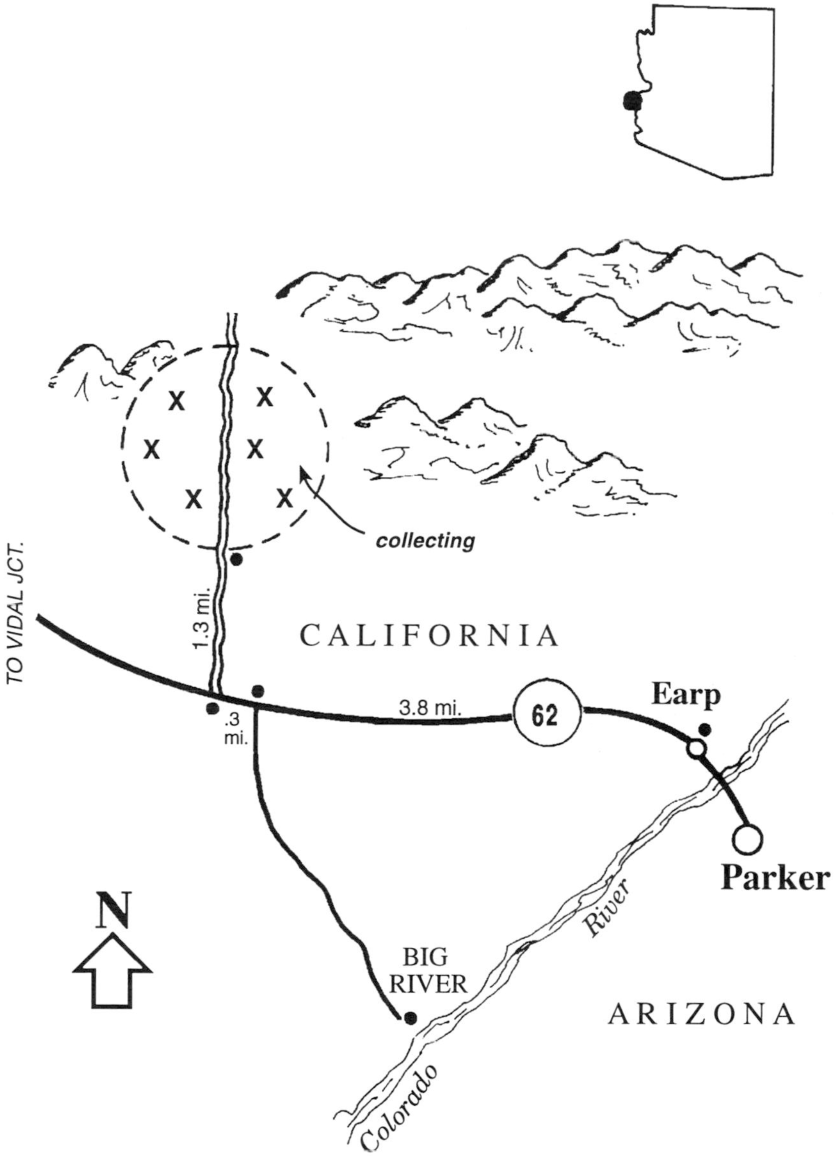

TO VIDAL JCT.

X X
X X
X X

collecting

1.3 mi.

CALIFORNIA

.3 mi.

3.8 mi.

62

Earp

Parker

N

BIG
RIVER

River

Colorado

ARIZONA

The region north of Carefree offers rockhounds six collecting opportunities, as shown on the map. Access to all of them is from Forest Road 24, reached by going six and one-half miles east from Carefree toward Horseshoe Lake. Bear left at the fork and go four and one-half miles to where a road intersects from the left, going up the hill to the Cave Creek Mistress Mine. This is actually a rock and souvenir shop built on the dumps. It serves as a good place to stop for updated information about the region, as well as providing an opportunity to see some local specimens.

Forest Road 254 intersects the main road six and two-tenths miles north of the Cave Creek Mistress Mine, and it is there where you should turn right and proceed about one-half mile. From there, scattered throughout the soil for quite a distance, is some of the most vivid red jasper imaginable. This is Site "A". Over the years much of the easily obtained material has been picked up, making it now necessary to do some patient hiking to the more difficult to reach regions, in order to gather good quantities. That, in fact, is the case for all of the Cave Creek sites.

Site "B" is just one and eight-tenths miles past the Cave Creek Campground and also features brilliant red jasper. Some of the specimens found at Site "B" are very interesting, filled with intricate patterns, including delicate white lace motifs. Again, nothing is overly plentiful near the road, so some walking will be necessary.

Site "C" is another two and one-tenth miles north, centered around the site of an old onyx mine. If the mine is not operating, colorful onyx can be gathered on the dumps. If the mine is closed, fairly good, but weathered, specimens can often be found in the wash below.

Site "D" is one and seven-tenths miles farther, and is reached by turning left and rounding the little hill to where the road is washed out. Small pieces of intricately patterned jasper and rhyolite can be gathered throughout the surrounding hills.

Site "E" features beautiful agate randomly strewn throughout the hills. The finest is found across the road at Site "F", which is the remnants of the Arizona Agate Mine. To reach the diggings, cross the stream and follow any of the numerous trails leading to the seams on the side of the cliff. Lots of spectacular agate can be picked up on the hillsides. The best is obtained by using a chisel, gad and sledge hammer to remove it from its place in the mountain. This involves tough work, but, keep in mind that it is also some of the most colorful agate available anywhere in Arizona.

CAVE CREEK AGATE & JASPER

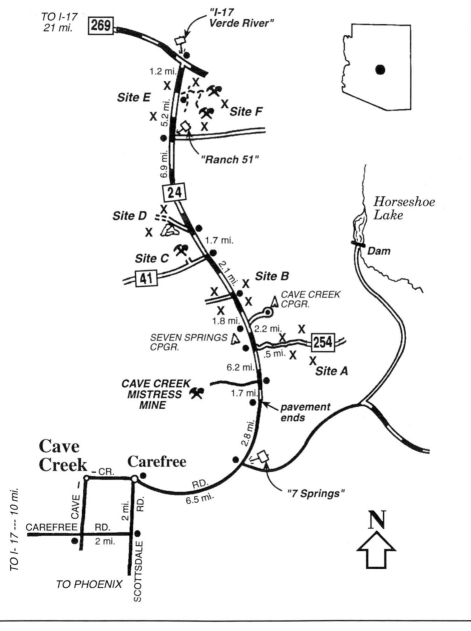

TO I-17
21 mi.

[269]

"I-17
Verde River"

1.2 mi.

Site E

X

X

5.2 mi.

X X **Site F**

X

X

6.9 mi.

"Ranch 51"

[24]

Horseshoe Lake

Site D

X

X

Dam

1.7 mi.

Site C

X

2.1 mi.

[41]

X X **Site B**

X X

CAVE CREEK
CPGR.

X

1.8 mi.

2.2 mi.

X

SEVEN SPRINGS
CPGR.

.5 mi.

X

[254]

X

6.2 mi.

Site A

**CAVE CREEK
MISTRESS
MINE**

1.7 mi.

pavement
ends

2.8 mi.

**Cave
Creek**

CR.

Carefree

RD.

6.5 mi.

"7 Springs"

CAVE

2 mi.

RD.

CAREFREE RD.

2 mi.

TO I-17 --- 10 mi.

SCOTTSDALE

TO PHOENIX

N

Site "A" provides an opportunity for mineral collectors to gather fluorite, quartz and feldspar crystals. Most are small, but, if many crystals can be found concentrated together, within a single specimen, the resulting piece can be worthy of display in a mineral collection.

To get there, take the road to Bartlett Lake out of Carefree and, after going six and one-half miles, bear right at the fork. From that point, drive another two and two-tenths miles, and carefully look for the very faint ruts leading off into the shallow hills, on the right. They are tough to spot until you are just about perpendicular to them, so be on the lookout. If you miss the turn, it is difficult to find a safe place to double back on this winding stretch of pavement. If your vehicle is capable, follow the rough and washed old road a few tenths of a mile to the old prospect. Search the weathered dumps and surrounding territory for mineral bearing rock. The best crystals are discovered by breaking up the dump material to expose fresh, unweathered surfaces.

To get to Site "B", return to the pavement, continue four and two-tenths more miles, and bear left another nine and one-half miles toward Horseshoe Lake. At that point Road 1063 leads off into the hills on the left, and it is there where you should turn. Go a few tenths of a mile, if your vehicle is capable, and search the hills and lowlands for agate, in a variety of colors and patterns. Some is white or light blue, while other is a shimmering translucent black. A few of the latter pieces contain brilliant red regions, which are the most prized from this locality.

In addition to agate, one can also pick up green, white, red, and orange jasper, all of which can be used to make beautiful polished pieces.

View of the collecting area from the road

HORSESHOE LAKE BLACK AGATE

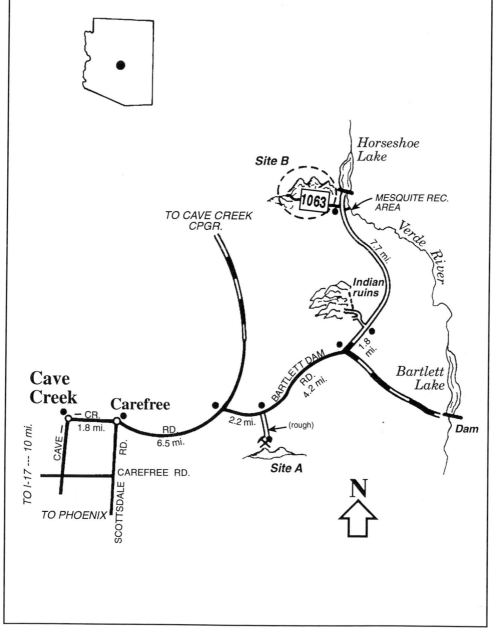

The hills and lowlands on both sides of the Verde River, in the vicinity of Sheep Crossing Bridge, offer rockhounds an excellent opportunity to gather colorful agate, jasper, and sagenite. This location is very remote, making it essential that you properly equip your vehicle for such a journey. It is also advisable to take along some extra supplies, especially something to drink, just in case you become delayed.

To get there, either take Forest Road 479 north from the Horseshoe Dam region, on the eastern side of the Verde River, or follow Forest Road 24 to Forest Road 269, as illustrated on the map. Both roads are graded, but rough in spots, so rugged vehicles are highly recommended.

The agate and jasper is found throughout the hills, on both sides of the river, especially on the east. The sagenite seems to be concentrated on top of the mesa just north of Forest Road 269, immediately before it winds its way down to the river.

Plan to do some walking in order to adequately explore the region. Always be on the lookout for rattlesnakes, especially during the warmer months. All of the material tends to be randomly scattered. Most of what can be obtained is good and solid, some filled with interesting inclusions, making them real prizes. This is a challenging place to collect, but the quality of what can be found, certainly helps to make up for that slight inconvenience.

Do not attempt wading across the Verde River, no matter how shallow and slow moving it appears. Always cross on the footbridge! The currents can be strong and dangerous. As refreshing as it might appear, a swim in the Verde would not be wise. It should also be noted that there are lots of great places to camp on the way to Sheep Crossing as well as alongside the river itself.

View of the lower collecting area

SHEEP CROSSING

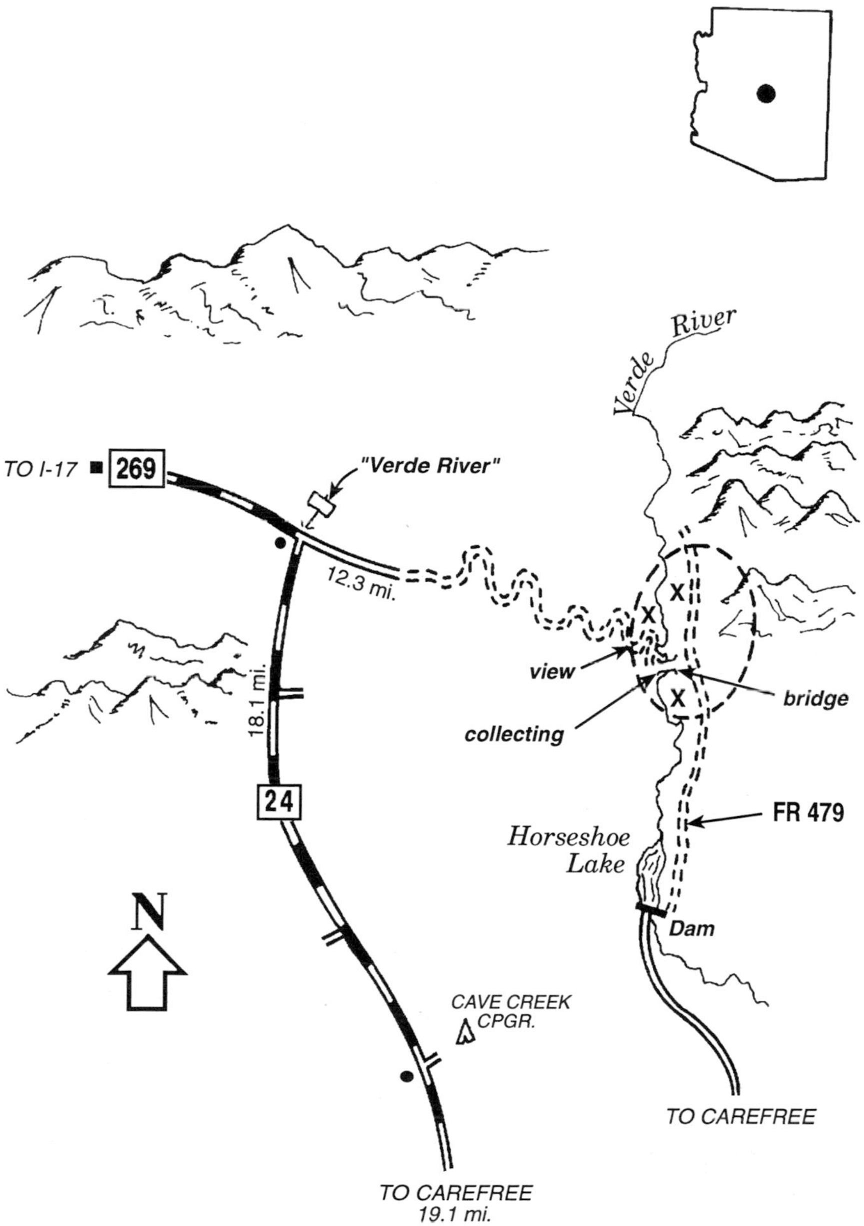

TO I-17 ■ **269**

"Verde River"

Verde River

12.3 mi.

18.1 mi.

24

X

X

view

collecting

bridge

FR 479

Horseshoe Lake

Dam

N

CAVE CREEK
CPGR.

TO CAREFREE

TO CAREFREE
19.1 mi.

There are three excellent sources of clean, bright-red jasper along the old road which once connected Cave Creek and New River. To get there from Cave Creek, go south on Cave Creek Road one and nine-tenths miles and then turn right onto New River Road. Continue, as illustrated on the map, one and two-tenths miles to where the road ends at a big wash. That is where the New River Bridge once stood.

From that point, it is necessary to park and hike, but the walk to Sites "A" and/or "B" isn't bad. If you make the trek in the warmer months, be on the lookout for ever present rattlesnakes, especially when scrambling over the boulders in the river bed.

Site "A" comprises the area just north of the New River wash, continuing up into the hills for quite a distance. There are some ruts paralleling the creek, on that side, which can be followed for easier access. The best collecting seems to be about three-tenths of a mile east along those ruts and continues at least another one-half mile. Search the surrounding areas for the brilliantly colored jasper and take time to select only the best, since some is very grainy.

Site "B" is only three-tenths of a mile farther north and is accessed by following the ruts leading east from the main road a few tenths of a mile, as illustrated. Red jasper is again scattered all over a wide area, in all directions.

Site "C", the final spot, is situated one and two-tenths miles farther. Due to the long hike involved, it may not be of interest, especially since it offers more of the same. If you choose to make the trek, there will be some steep tracks leading right from the main road. Follow them one and two-tenths miles farther, bearing right at the fork. The red jasper, some of which is nearly purple, can be found all along the ruts as well as scattered throughout the lowlands.

NEW RIVER RED JASPER

Site C

1.2 mi.

1.2 mi.

TO NEW RIVER

Site B

.3 mi.

Site A

New River wash

bridge out

.3 mi.

NEW RIVER RD.

.9 mi.

"New River Rd."

Cave
Creek

TO CAREFREE --- 2mi.

1.9 mi.

RD.

.6 mi.

TO I-17
10 mi.

CAREFREE RD.

CAVE CREEK

N

TO PHOENIX

Very nice, fine grained, red and green marble can be collected in the shadows of the spectacular Superstition Mountains, not far from the town of Queen Valley. To get to this most productive location, go north on Queen Valley Road one and seven-tenths miles from where it intersects Highway 60. From there, turn right onto Hewitt Station Road, go three and three-tenths miles and then proceed north onto Forest Road 172.

Some stretches of the Forest Road are rough, so a rugged vehicle will be needed to make it all the way. Continue four and three-tenths miles and ruts will be encountered branching off to the right, into a shallow canyon. Follow those ruts one-half mile or as far as your vehicle is capable of going. There is lots of loose sand. Unless you have four-wheel drive, it might be advisable to hike the rest of the way to the marble deposit rather than ride in your vehicle.

The site is easily spotted since it is an old quarry. Good samples of marble are scattered all over, directly below the mine and throughout the adjacent wash. Most collectors are satisfied with what can be procured from the rubble below the workings, but some like to tackle the seam itself with gads, bars and chisels. Granted, some beautiful material can be extracted using hard rock methods, but it is tough work. If you choose to attack the seam itself, be sure to wear gloves and goggles and have plenty on hand to drink.

Seam at the collecting site

QUEEN VALLEY MARBLE

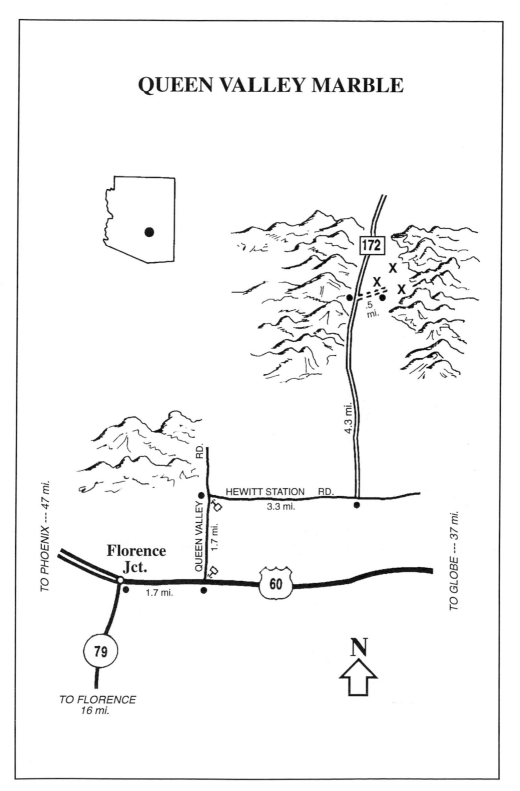

172

.5 mi.

4.3 mi.

RD.

QUEEN VALLEY

HEWITT STATION   RD.
3.3 mi.

1.7 mi.

TO PHOENIX --- 47 mi.

Florence Jct.

1.7 mi.

60

TO GLOBE --- 37 mi.

79

TO FLORENCE
16 mi.

N

Some of the finest Apache tears available anywhere come from a deposit southwest of Superior. At one time this was a fee location and collectors simply had to show up, pay the fee, and start gathering the little gems. Now, however, the site is being mined for its perlite and is closed, except to those able to get special permission. Obviously, rockhounds cannot enter the area when the miners are working. Weekends seem to be the only days available, and even weekends are sometimes impossible.

At time of publication, collecting information could be obtained by calling (602) 689-5723 or by visiting the office at Nord Perlite Company, on the north side of Highway 60, as shown on the map. It is strongly recommended that you make collecting arrangements before your visit. Contacting the appropriate people is sometimes difficult and there seems to be some inconsistency related to regulations governing the property.

To get to this famous location, take Highway 60 west from Superior approximately one mile. Just before reaching the given mileage, you will see the large Superior Waste Water Management Plant sign. Turn south, just past that sign, and proceed one and three-tenths miles to the gate and the "No Trespassing" sign.

At the quarry, it seems that there are Apache tears just about everywhere, ranging in size from less than a quarter of an inch in diameter to some as large as an egg, and it won't take much time to gather hundreds of them. Be sure to also get a few specimens still embedded in the host perlite, since those make outstanding display pieces just the way they are.

The perlite, which is the predominant material here, is a fibrous volcanic glass, making it imperative that you be careful not to rub your eyes or face until washing your hands.

Gathering Apache tears

SUPERIOR APACHE TEARS

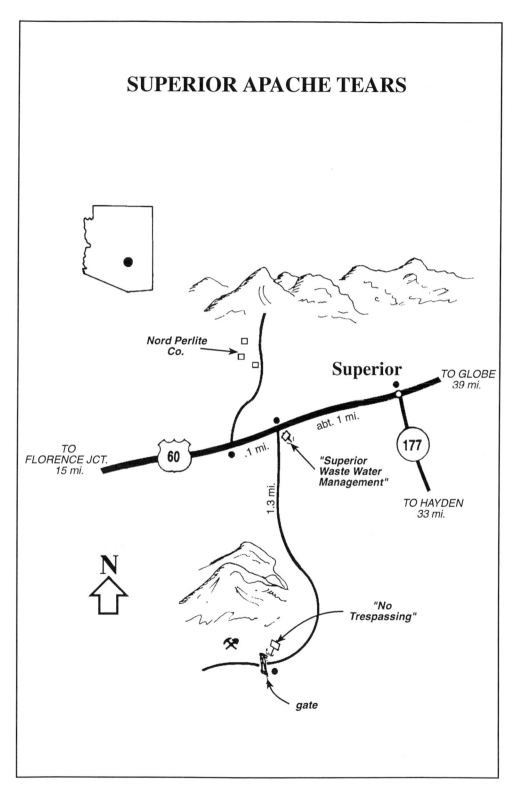

Nord Perlite Co.

Superior

TO GLOBE 39 mi.

TO FLORENCE JCT. 15 mi.

60

abt. 1 mi.

.1 mi.

177

"Superior Waste Water Management"

TO HAYDEN 33 mi.

1.3 mi.

N

"No Trespassing"

gate

The mines discussed here are not necessarily open to collecting. Generally, when they are available to rockhounds, some sort of prior arrangement needs to be made. The region is discussed primarily because of its mineralogical significance, and as a place that anyone interested in Arizona minerals would most surely want to visit.

A drive through these towns, past the colossal dumps, is extremely interesting. It is fascinating to see where some of the most beautiful copper specimens in the word have come from. These mines are noted for their incredibly beautiful azurite, chrysocolla, malachite and native copper. There isn't a museum in the world that wouldn't want to display some of those brilliantly colored specimens.

If you want to attempt collecting on some of the dumps, keep in mind that it is usually only possible to do so on weekends, and it is often essential that you be a part of a group or club. Single rockhounds or very small groups will have difficulty gaining admittance, primarily for insurance reasons and the cost of escorting such a limited number of people to the approved collecting spots.

To inquire about tours or collecting, contact any of the mines directly, or consult the major lapidary /mineral magazines for listings of clubs in the region which could provide good information about field trips and other up-to-date local collecting regulations.

Two major mining companies in the Superior / Globe locale are the Phelps Dodge Corp., 2600 N. Central Ave., Phoenix, AZ 85004, (602) 234-8100, and the Magma Copper Co., P.O. Box 100, Miami, AZ 85539, (602) 473-6200.

One of the numerous mines between Superior and Globe

COPPER COUNTRY

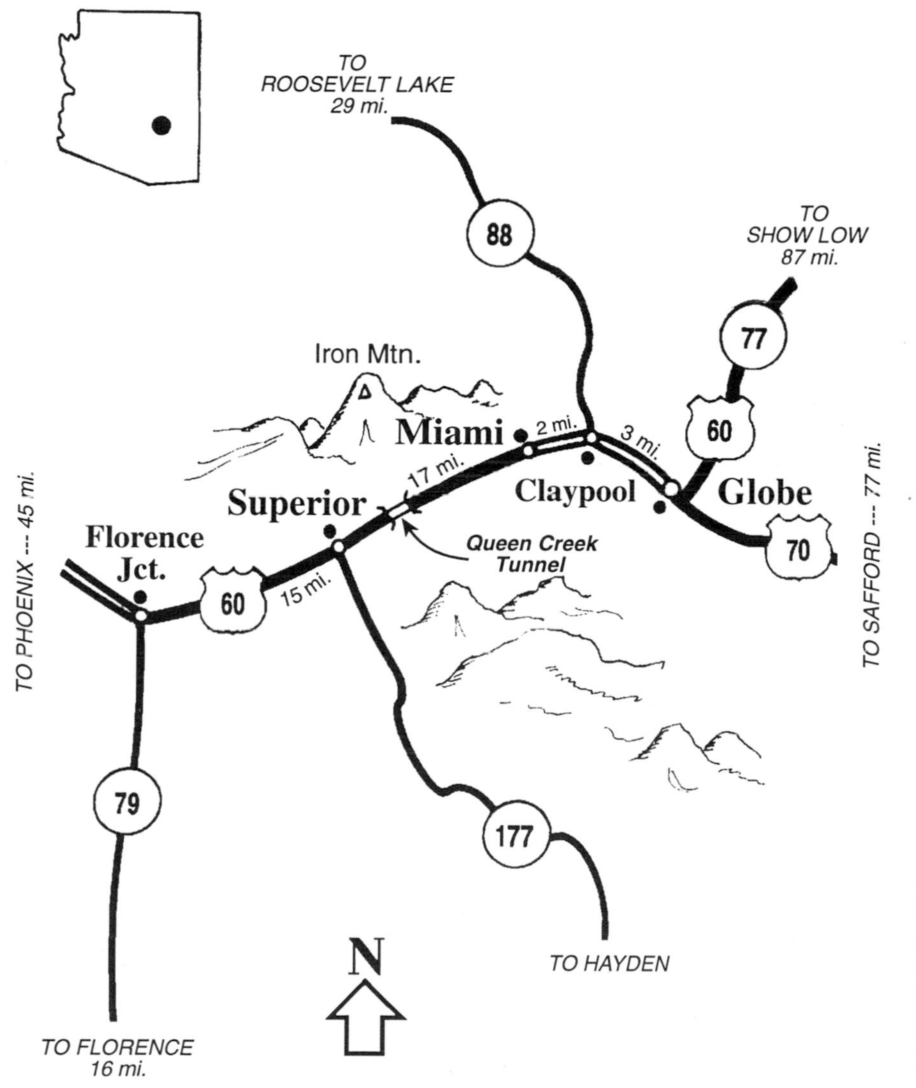

TO
ROOSEVELT LAKE
29 mi.

88

TO
SHOW LOW
87 mi.

77

Iron Mtn.

60

Miami

2 mi.

3 mi.

TO PHOENIX --- 45 mi.

17 mi.

Superior

Claypool

Globe

Florence
Jct.

60

Queen Creek
Tunnel

TO SAFFORD --- 77 mi.

70

15 mi.

79

177

N

TO HAYDEN

TO FLORENCE
16 mi.

Some of the most colorful onyx available anywhere in Arizona comes from a deposit located in the mountains north of Globe. To get there, take Highway 60/77 north from town sixteen and one-half miles. Just as you pass the bridge over Seven Mile Wash, there will be a road heading to the west. From there, follow the instructions on the map to the collecting area. As you approach the proper mileage, look for the little turnout on the left. There isn't much room for more than a few cars, but it is the best place to park near the onyx deposit.

It will then be necessary to hike north, up the hill, to the small, partially overgrown onyx quarry. It isn't a bad trek, and using the old mine road is much easier than cross country hiking directly up the hillside through the thorn bushes and brush. There is a hard to see post designating the old mine road as Road 1973. It is not passable by any but the most rugged four-wheel drive units.

Colors vary from near solid white, to pieces swirled and/or layered with red, pink, white, gray and yellow. Plenty of this top quality onyx can be found scattered all over the hillside below the seam itself and most collectors are satisfied with what can be gathered from that material. Incredibly beautiful pieces, however, can also be removed from their place in the mountain with gads, chisels and pry bars. This is tough work though, but the rewards for the labor are often worth it. Be sure to wear goggles when directly working the seam.

A portion of the onyx seam

GLOBE ONYX

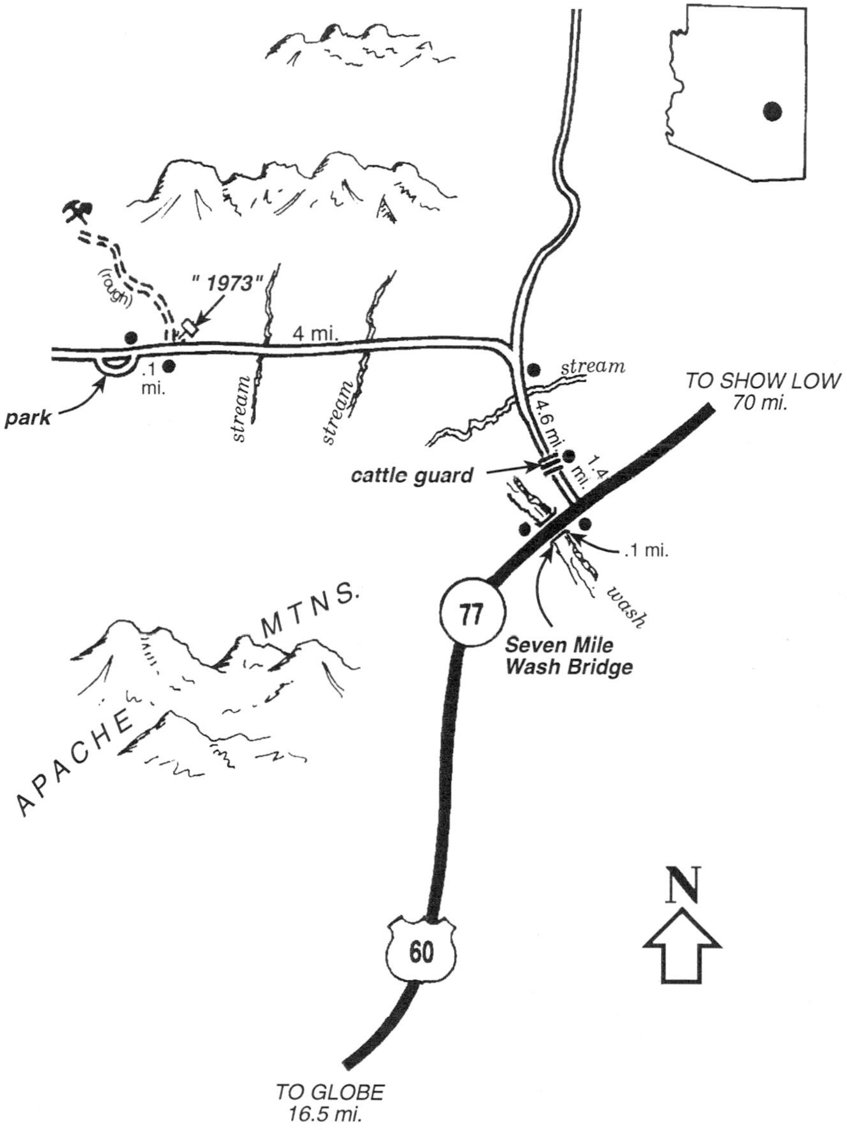

"1973"

4 mi.

stream

park

.1 mi.

stream

stream

stream

.4.6 mi.

cattle guard

.1.4 mi.

TO SHOW LOW
70 mi.

77

wash

.1 mi.

Seven Mile
Wash Bridge

A P A C H E   M T N S.

60

N

TO GLOBE
16.5 mi.

This easy to reach site is designated as the Black Hills Rockhound Area by the Bureau of Land Management and is maintained expressly for the benefit of mineral collectors.

To get to the fire agate field, go ten miles east of Safford, on Highway 70, to Highway 191, and then proceed northeast ten and one-half miles to milepost 141. The turnoff is just three-tenths of a mile farther, on the left, as shown on the map. Go through the cattle guard and follow the ranch road about one and one-half miles. It is a fairly good gravel road, but passenger cars may find it difficult in spots. Cross a small wash and then climb to the campground and collecting area.

Chalcedony can be found scattered all over the landscape, stretching for quite a distance. The prime material of interest here is, of course, the brownish chalcedony, exhibiting colorful fire. It won't take long to find pieces with traces of brown and gold, indicating the potential for fire. Most of what is picked up will not contain the highly desirable bursts of color. Be patient and willing to do some exploring, however, and you should be able to gather a few of the gemstones.

The best success is generally attained by climbing the little mountain to the east of the registration sign or roaming the nearby hills. Chalcedony litters the ground, and some is still embedded in the mountain where it was formed. Either directly work the deposits or pick up specimens from float. Digging and screening the soil also provides the potential for finding worthwhile material. If you do dig, though, fill your holes when done.

Return to the highway and continue to Thumb Butte, on the south. In the area around that prominent landmark, as well as in surrounding washes, collectors can find small agate nodules, petrified palm root, and Apache tears.

Leaving the Black Hills rock hounding area

BLACK HILLS FIRE AGATE

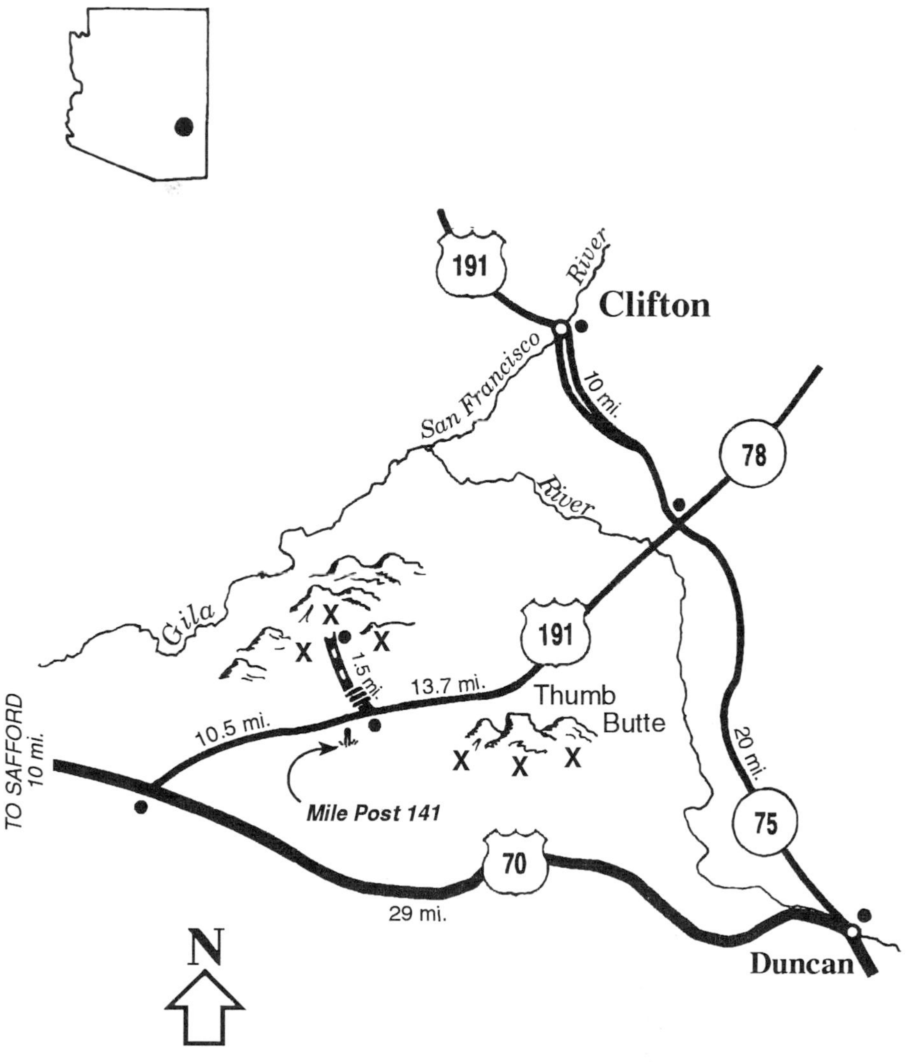

191

San Francisco River

Clifton

10 mi.

78

River

191

13.7 mi.

Thumb
Butte

X X

X X X

Gila

X
X
X

1.5 mi.

10.5 mi.

Mile Post 141

TO SAFFORD
10 mi.

70

29 mi.

20 mi.

75

Duncan

N

The region surrounding prominent Mulligan Peak, northeast of Clifton, boasts frequently large agate nodules and geodes. The agate is often intricately banded with beautiful fortification patterns. Colors range from deep purple to lavender and gray. Chips and pieces are scattered all over the area.

The large nodules are primarily obtained by digging them from the ground like potatoes. They occur just under the top soil, and some are still in place within the host rhyolite where they formed.

This is not an easy area to reach (see map). To get there from Clifton, take the SECOND bridge crossing the San Francisco River, bear left, and go about two miles to the entrance of Limestone Canyon. From there, four-wheel drive is probably necessary, since the ruts weave in and out of a sandy wash.

The first trail leading to the digging area exits the Limestone Canyon road after about one-half mile, and is on the right. It is tough to spot, so be sure to watch closely as you approach the given mileage.

The trail leads up the steep slopes to Mulligan Peak's southwest side and the trek is tough. At trail's end you should be able to see where others have dug before. Look for pieces of agate and other debris as indicators as to where you should start.

There is another collecting area on the opposite side of the mountain and it is reached by continuing along the the road in Limestone Canyon approximately one more mile. At that point, you should see the remnants of an old cabin and a gate. Go through the gate and follow the road that branches to the right.

You will encounter some water troughs and pipes and eventually a very large boulder on the side of the hill with a trail leading toward it. That marks the center of the agate field. As before, some material will be found on the surface, but the best is usually obtained by digging.

Be sure to carry plenty of water, since this is a long and arduous hike and the temperature can get very hot.

CLIFTON AGATE

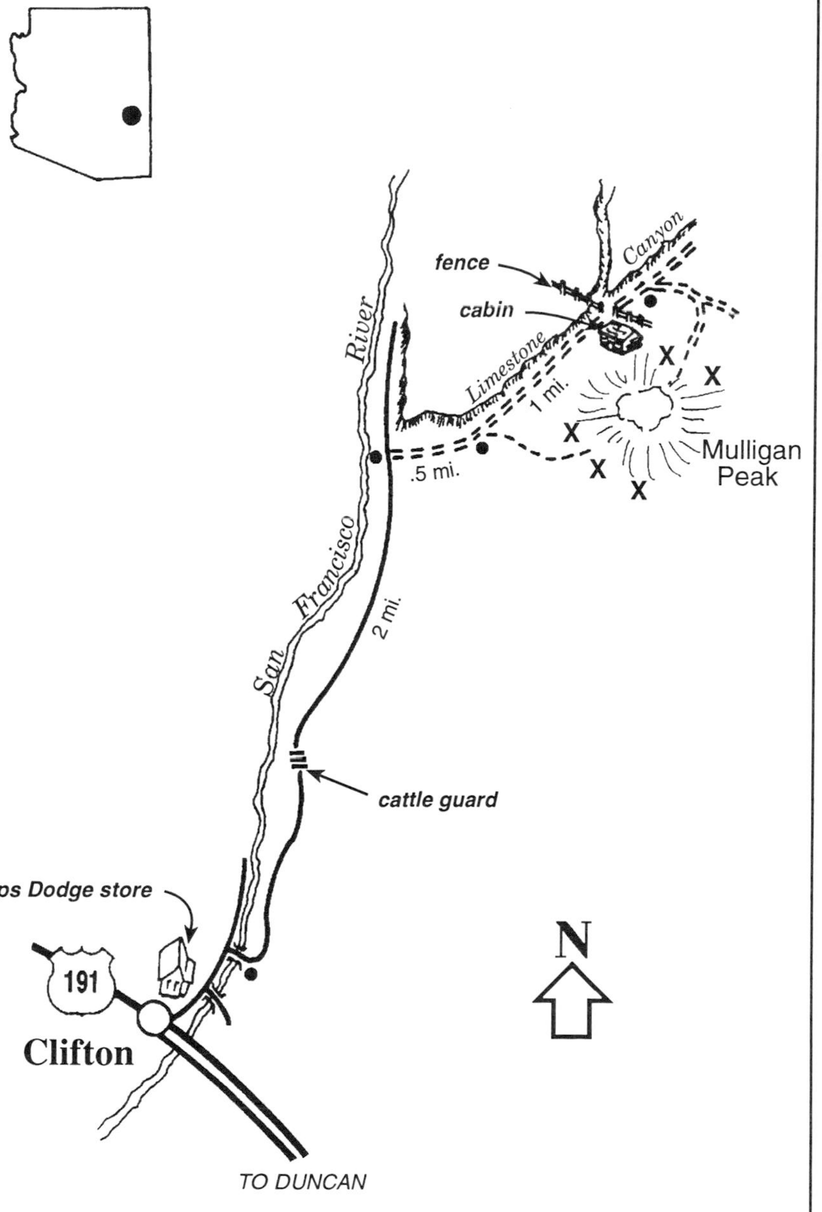

fence

cabin

Canyon

River

Limestone

1 mi.

.5 mi.

San Francisco

2 mi.

X **X** **X**

X **X**

X

Mulligan Peak

cattle guard

Phelps Dodge store

191

Clifton

N

TO DUNCAN

These sites offer collectors plume and flower agate, as well as chalcedony and precious fire agate. To get to the wash, which marks the first location, take Highway 191 to the exit at the school situated on the southern edge of Clifton. From there, go under the bridge, as shown on the map, proceed five miles to a fork, bear left and continue another six-tenths of a mile. Instead of heading into Loma Linda Estates, go right, down the hill, to where a wash crosses the road. It is in and around that wash where one can find the chalcedony, some of which is filled with fire.

Common chalcedony is fairly plentiful here, especially if you are willing to hike a distance up or down the wash, and much contains areas of brown and/or orange, indicating a potential for fire. Shimmering, color-filled fire agate, however, is not abundant. It takes lots of patience and determination to find much. Carry a canteen of water or a moist rag to wet suspicious stones. The wetting helps bring out the fire, if there is any. As you walk through the wash, don't hesitate to rake through the soft sand or move some boulders. It is in places like those that prize specimens can be hidden.

To get to the other two sites from the wash, follow the road up the hill for about one and four-tenths miles to a gate. Search there for desert roses and agate. Another two and eight-tenths miles places you next to a little hill. The terrain surrounding that hill is randomly littered with chalcedony, agate, and crystals. The agate comes in a variety of colors with numerous interesting inclusions, including some exhibiting exquisite plume and/or flower patterns. Most is small and nothing here is overly plentiful.

CLIFTON FIRE AGATE

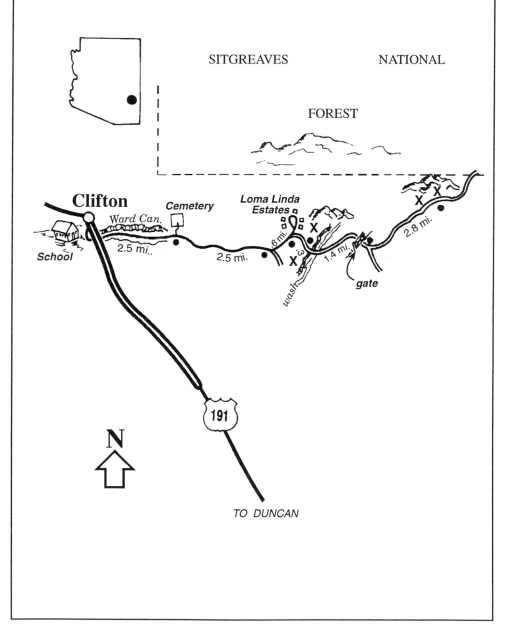

SITGREAVES   NATIONAL

FOREST

Clifton

Cemetery

Loma Linda
Estates

School

Ward Can.

2.5 mi..

2.5 mi.

.6 mi.

X

X

.3

wash

1.4 mi.

gate

X   X

2.8 mi.

191

N

TO DUNCAN

Good quality Apache tears always seem to be in demand by rockhounds. This location provides an opportunity to find lots of small, generally opaque, specimens. These can be tumbled, made into beautiful cabochons, or faceted.

To get there, take Highway 78 to the state line, about fifteen miles northeast from where it intersects Highway 75. There is a turnout, on the south, just past the Arizona/New Mexico border. The Apache tears can be found scattered everywhere throughout the trees, on both sides of the road. Be certain to pull well off the pavement and be cautious when crossing the highway.

No camping is allowed at this site, but the tiny parking area does provide a great spot for a lunch stop. From wherever you choose to park, it will be necessary to crawl under the highway fence in order to have access to the complete Apache tear field. If you do decide to go to the opposite side, be certain not to damage the fence.

This collecting site is particularly nice during the summer months when you can roam through the cool shade of the pine trees as you look for the beautiful black gemstones. Winters, however, can get quite cold. The best time of day to search for Apache tears is in the early morning or late afternoon. Keep the sun to your back and the glass-like tears will catch the sun's rays and sparkle as you walk.

Parked at the collecting site

MULE CREEK APACHE TEARS

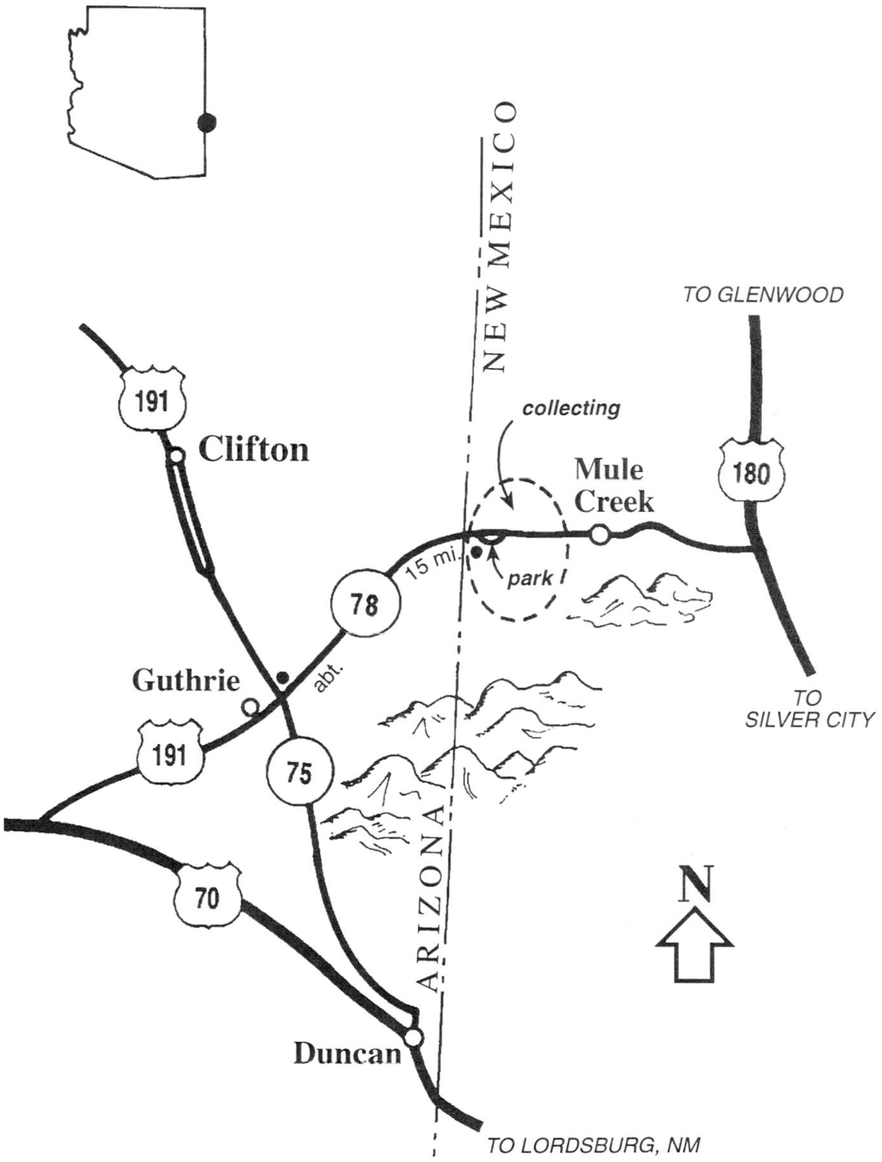

NEW MEXICO

ARIZONA

TO GLENWOOD

191

Clifton

180

collecting

Mule
Creek

15 mi.

78

park !

Guthrie

abt.

TO
SILVER CITY

191

75

TO SAFFORD

70

N

Duncan

TO LORDSBURG, NM

This location, situated a short distance east of the Arizona border, in New Mexico, is noted for its fine geodes and nodules. To get there, start in Douglas at the intersection of Highway 80 and Fifteenth Street. Go east on Fifteenth Street a short distance out of town, until it becomes the Geronimo Trail (Forest Road 63).

The road soon turns to gravel and then dirt. You should proceed across the desert thirty-two miles to the western edge of Coronado National Forest. Three more miles brings you to the New Mexico border. The collecting commences about two miles further, throughout Clanton Draw. The road is well maintained, but it goes through some desolate country and there are no services along the way. Be sure you have plenty of gasoline, your vehicle is in good working order, and you take along some extra supplies, in the event you become delayed.

The geodes can be found in areas of erosion, roadcuts, and even lying on the road, for approximately ten more miles. The best concentrations seem to be within the three-mile stretch illustrated on the map. Be on the lookout for freshly graded soil or mounds of dirt just off the road, since such areas tend to contain geodes and nodules.

It is also suggested that you randomly stop just about anywhere and search the hills and washes in an attempt to gather more sizable specimens. A good mode of collecting is to first find regions on or beside the road that contain indications of geodes or nodules and, from there, explore the surrounding countryside.

The geodes and nodules tend to be brownish-red, but range in color from tan to almost orange. Be advised that lots of interesting, bubbly chalcedony is also scattered throughout this area, as is some very nice agate.

GERONIMO TRAIL GEODES

TO
ROADS FORKS, NM
& I-10

TO ANIMAS
32 mi.

338

NEW MEXICO

ARIZONA

N

80

collecting

7 mi.

CORONADO

3 mi.

2 mi.

3 mi.

NAT'L

FOREST

TR.

32 mi.

GERONIMO

63

Douglas

TO BISBEE

MEXICO

The dumps of the old Carlyle Mine provide rockhounds with amethyst, pyrite cubes, and a host of other minerals. It is a rough journey to the collecting site, and the trip should only be attempted in rugged vehicles.

To get there, take Highway 75 north from Duncan one and one-tenth miles to Carlyle Road and turn east, off the pavement. Proceed another thirteen and one-half miles into the mountains to where a mine dump will be encountered on the left. At that point, there is also a sign designating this to now be Summit Peak Road, and tracks lead off to the right toward the central mining area.

At time of publication, there was some active mining being done in the region. For safety reasons, permission was required before doing any collecting. To obtain that consent, go to the office, as shown on the map. If nobody is there, search only on unposted dumps along Summit Peak Road.

Remember that old dumps can be very dangerous, making it essential to always be on the lookout for abandoned pits covered with decaying timbers, broken glass and rusty nails.

Continuing along Summit Peak Road, you will encounter numerous additional dumps, any one of which offers good collecting possibilities. At the three and one-half mile mark, lots of colorful jasper, chert and agate can be found scattered throughout the washes and flatlands. The highway can be reached by continuing along this road thirteen more miles, bearing left at major forks.

An old dump at the jasper mine

CARLYLE MINE DUMPS

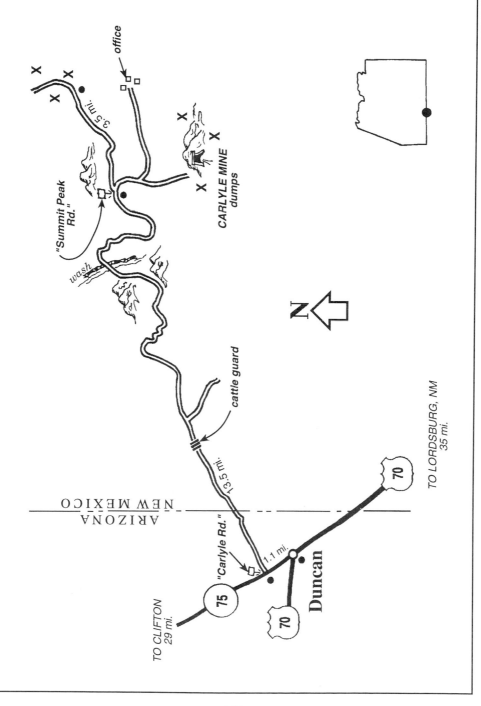

office

X X
X

3.5 mi.

X
X
CARLYLE MINE
dumps
X

"Summit Peak
Rd."

wash

N

cattle guard

TO LORDSBURG, NM
35 mi.

13.5 mi.

ARIZONA
NEW MEXICO

70

"Carlyle Rd."

1.1 mi.

75

Duncan

70

TO CLIFTON
29 mi.

This area features chalcedony roses and beautiful fire agate. To get there from Duncan, head south on Highway 70, about twelve miles, to milepost 5. From there, the turnoff is only six-tenths of a mile farther. At the proper mileage, go west, and proceed six and eight-tenths miles to where a BLM sign instructs you to turn left. From that point, rugged vehicles are recommended, since the road is not regularly maintained and could be rough in places. Be sure to bring plenty of water and gas, since it is a most remote area.

After having gone about two and one-half miles, chalcedony can be found all along the road, and it might be worth your time to stop and do a little searching. This is labeled as Site "A" on the map. The boundary of the primary location, Site "B", however, is another two and one-half miles farther along. At that point, a cattle guard and gate will be encountered. Go through the gate and follow the loop road around the mountain to what is generally regarded as the most productive of the Round Mountain collecting areas. This is probably because few people get that far due to the roughness of the road.

Walk throughout the flatlands, paying particularly close attention to any brown or gold chalcedony. It won't take much time to locate such pieces, which have the most potential for exhibiting the beautiful and highly prized fire. Be patient and willing to spend sufficient time here and you should be rewarded with some spectacular gemstones.

BLM sign near the entrance of the Round Mountain area

ROUND MOUNTAIN FIRE AGATE

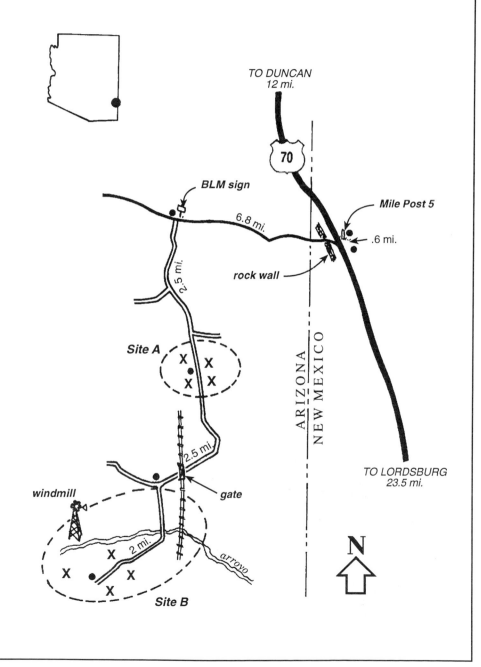

TO DUNCAN
12 mi.

70

BLM sign

6.8 mi.

Mile Post 5

.6 mi.

rock wall

2.5 mi.

Site A

X   X
X X

ARIZONA
NEW MEXICO

2.5 mi.

gate

windmill

2 mi.

arroyo

TO LORDSBURG
23.5 mi.

X
X   X
X

Site B

N

Lots of agate and chalcedony can be gathered at this somewhat remote location, as well as color-filled fire agate. To get there, go south from Duncan about nineteen miles to milepost 12, continue seven-tenths of a mile farther, and then turn left. Proceed on that graded dirt road ten and nine-tenth miles to a fork. Bear right at the fork, continuing seven-tenths of a mile to the start of this extensive and highly productive region. The last stretch is rough, and a rugged vehicle will probably be necessary.

When you stop, whether it be at the given mileage or anywhere from that point all the way to the mountains, about two miles farther west, you will be amazed at the amount of agate and chalcedony that will be encountered. The finest agate is a delicately banded pink hue which can be used to produce exquisite cabochons. Beautiful, well-formed, bubbly chalcedony roses are also quite easy to find and they are occasionally covered with tiny quartz crystals. There are also some chalcedony geodes scattered about, but they tend to be quite small.

You will notice that much of the chalcedony has regions of dark brown and orange, which indicates the potential for fire. Be on the lookout for gold/brown, bubbly pieces, since they could be real prizes. Be sure to allow enough time to explore as much of this vast area as possible. It is a relatively new location and not much surface collection has taken place.

Searching the collecting area for specimens

DUNCAN FIRE AGATE

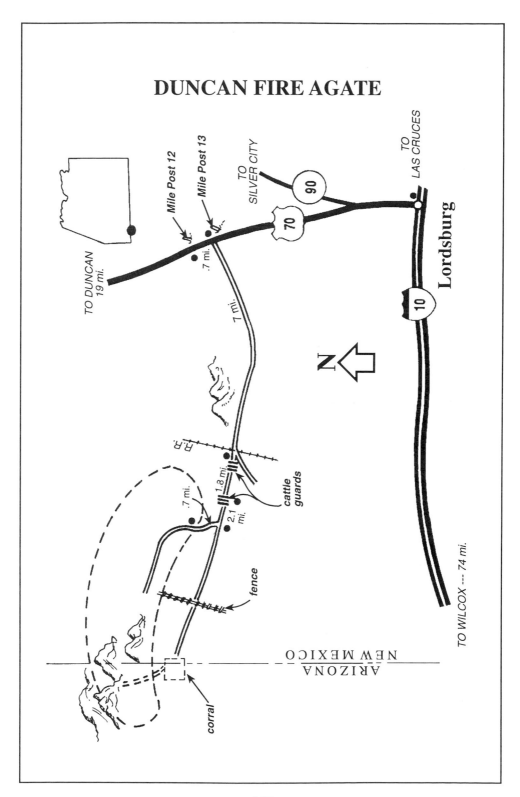

At one time, this well respected chalcedony and fire agate location was maintained by the Bureau of Land Management for the exclusive use of rockhounds. That government agency, however, gave up the responsibility a number of years ago, due to the site's remoteness, the expense of maintaining the road, and the limited number of visitors each year. Access is still available, though, and it remains productive.

To get there from Bowie, go north on Central Avenue one and eight-tenths miles and then turn right onto Fan Road. From there, follow the instructions of the map another twenty-one and eight-tenths miles to the base of the hills. The road is not bad, and most rugged vehicles shouldn't have any problem going all the way.

The collecting area is extensive, covering many acres. There is a loop road which will take you near the mountains. Chalcedony, some of which contains fire, can be found by stopping just about anywhere along that road. The best pieces tend to be found nearer the mountains, away from the road. It seems that most people who collect here do what is easiest and search close to their vehicles, making distant spots more productive.

The terrain is generally flat, thereby providing some great places for a dry camp, if you choose to spend a few days here.

Information stop on the way into Joy Valley

JOY VALLEY FIRE AGATE

corral

4.6 mi.

gate

4.9 mi.

.9 mi.

corral

metal fence & gate

1.2 mi.

cattle guards

N

4.2 mi.

3.5 mi.

CENTRAL AVE.

2 mi.

FAN RD.

1.8 mi.

R.R.

TO WILCOX --- 12 mi.

TO LORDSBURG, NM --- 48 mi.

10

Exit 362

Exit 366

Bowie

This is an interesting area and it will probably take more than one day to adequately explore all of its collecting opportunities. The mountains near Courtland, Gleeson and Pearce, as illustrated on the map, are littered with old mine dumps. Many of these are abandoned and offer rockhounds a good chance to find a variety of minerals including wulfenite, aurichalcite, pyrite, bornite, chrysocolla and rosasite. In fact, some of the best bornite (peacock ore) to be found anywhere can be gathered from the dumps just north of Gleeson.

Near Courtland is a turquoise mine which was operated by Tiffanies in the 1880s. The material found there was beautiful and the mine is still operated sporadically. If interested in visiting this once prosperous prospect, inquiry at the Pearce store may provide information in regard to current status.

Another area of interest is Sugar Loaf Mountain, near the road to Elfrida. Hunt for agate, green quartz, geodes and crystal-filled geode pieces along the southern slopes.

Be careful when exploring abandoned mine dumps, since the associated terrain is often filled with hidden pits, shafts, rusty nails and broken glass. In addition, never enter a tunnel in this mining district. Many are flooded and the rock is rotten. There is still some mining being conducted in the locality, so do not trespass onto any private areas.

A good place from which to base your exploration of this once rich mining district is in nearby Tombstone, where there are campgrounds and motels.

Remnant of old building within the collecting area

GLEESON AREA MINERALS

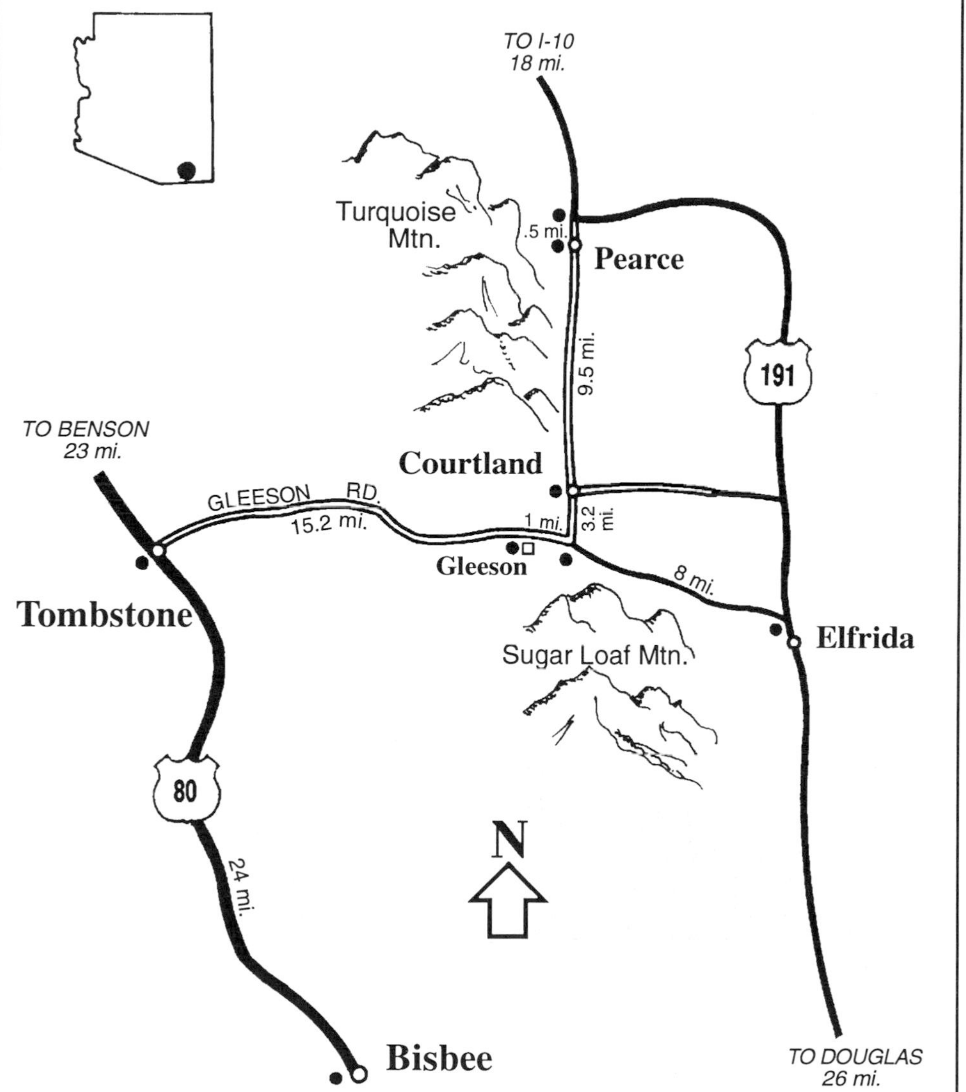

TO I-10
18 mi.

Turquoise Mtn.

.5 mi.

Pearce

9.5 mi.

191

TO BENSON
23 mi.

GLEESON RD.
15.2 mi.

Courtland

1 mi.

3.2 mi.

Gleeson

8 mi.

Tombstone

Sugar Loaf Mtn.

Elfrida

80

24 mi.

N

Bisbee

TO DOUGLAS
26 mi.

This is an easy area to reach, and features intriguing, bladed selenite balls, as well as lots of other interesting minerals, including a colorful variety of banded rhyolite.

To get there from Benson, take Highway 80 four and nine-tenths miles south from town to Apache Powder Plant Road, which intersects on the right, just as the highway curves to the left. Follow Apache Powder Plant Road three and one-half miles, turn right onto the ruts, go one-half mile, then proceed left toward the hills another six-tenths of a mile, and park. The last stretch is sandy in spots, but rugged vehicles should have no problems.

Stop just about anywhere near the sand hills and randomly explore them. The rhyolite is easy to see, being very colorful, but the selenite is much the same hue as the surrounding soil, making it more difficult to spot.

Generally, the selenite is found in the red-brown regions and digging into the soft soil is the best way to get the choicest pieces. You should be able to find lots of small selenite roses and stars, but sizable ones are more rare.

Be careful when digging, since the selenite roses and stars are very fragile, especially when first exposed to the air.

The hills are quite extensive, and it would probably be worthwhile to inspect as large a portion as possible. Sections of the hills located farther from the access roads will tend to be less picked over and thereby offer better potential for finding a greater supply of quality minerals.

Selenite roses of all sizes can be found near St. David

ST. DAVID SELENITE CLUSTERS

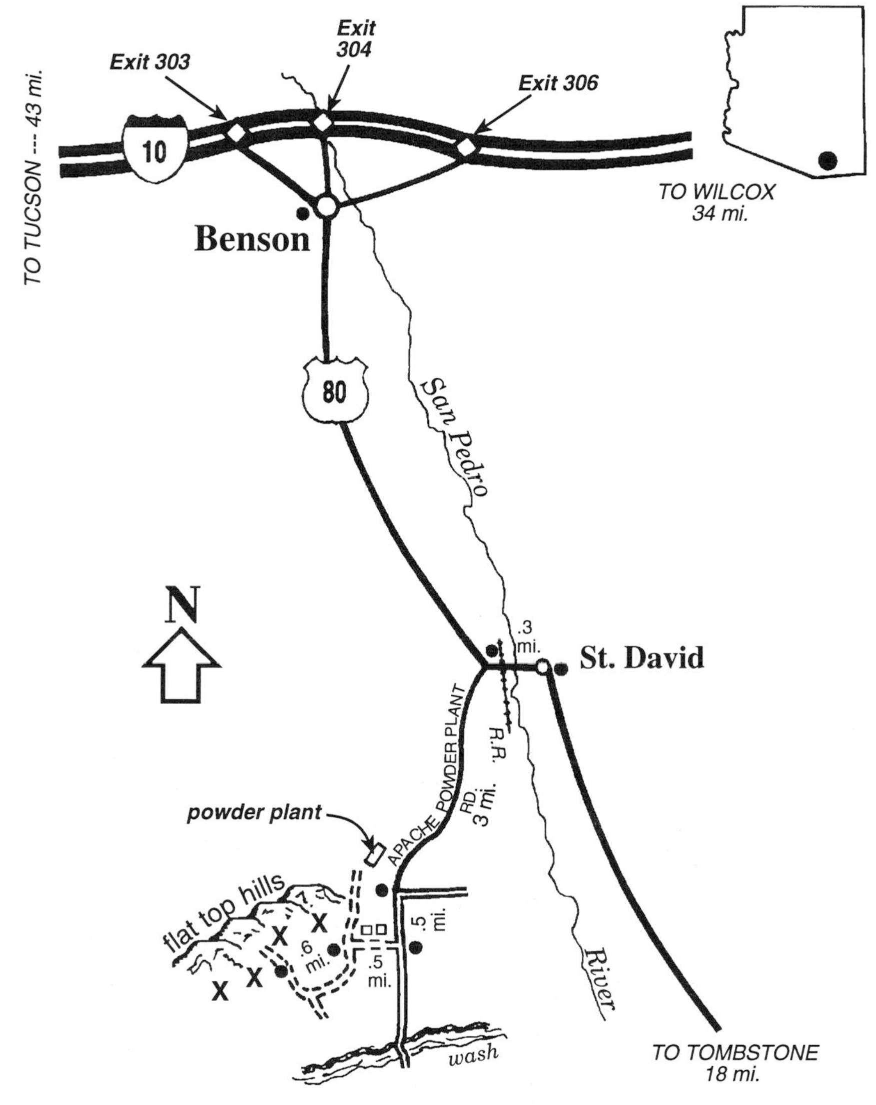

TO TUCSON --- 43 mi.

Exit 303

Exit 304

Exit 306

10

TO WILCOX
34 mi.

Benson

80

San Pedro

N

.3
mi.

St. David

R.R.

APACHE POWDER PLANT

RD.
3 mi.

powder plant

flat top hills

.6
mi.

.5
mi.

.5
mi.

River

wash

TO TOMBSTONE
18 mi.

Not far from bustling Tucson are the rugged Santa Catalina Mountains, and, nestled within some of the northern canyons, are regions of fossil-filled limestone. The location described here is just one of many such fossil bearing sites in the Santa Catalina Mountains, and one of the easiest to visit.

To get there, take Interstate 10 north from town, about five miles, to the Prince Road offramp (Exit 254). Go east one and nine-tenths miles, and turn left onto Highway 77, which is called Miracle Mile, at that point. Drive north twenty and four-tenths miles, and then bear east at Oracle Junction another nine and one-tenth miles, to where Oracle Road intersects from the right.

Proceed through the tiny town of Oracle and go right onto the Mt. Lemmon Highway, as illustrated on the map. After having gone ten and six-tenths miles from Highway 77, you will find yourself at Peppersauce Campground, and you should park just west of where Forest Road 38 and Forest Road 29 intersect.

From there, hike about 100 yards to where a small wash intersects the road. Follow that wash to the left, as it goes up the hill, for about fifteen yards, to the beginning of the fossil-bearing limestone deposit. It is in and around that gray limestone where you should conduct your search.

The Devonian fossils, including coral, shells, trilobites and crinoid stems, were deposited nearly 400 million years ago. It takes some careful examination of the limestone to spot the partially exposed fossils, but once you discover a few, subsequent specimens are much easier to find.

You may want to break away chunks of the tough rock directly from the deposit itself. That probably won't be necessary, since there are many manageably-sized pieces strewn throughout the little wash and surrounding hillsides. When you find limestone that seems to contain a good number of fossils, it is suggested that you save it for a location better suited to careful trimming, so you can expose the embedded fossils with minimal damage.

If you would like to spend some time in the area, Peppersauce Campground is a convenient place to set up camp.

TUCSON FOSSILS

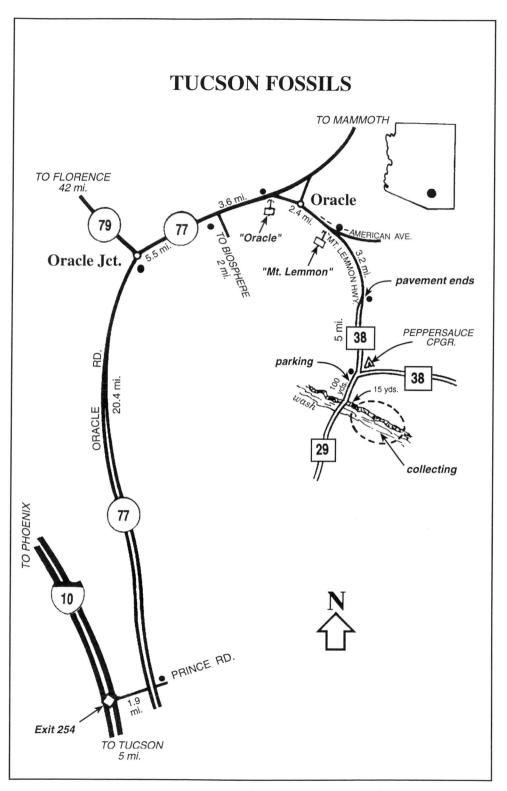

TO MAMMOTH

TO FLORENCE
42 mi.

79

77

3.6 mi.

"Oracle"

Oracle

2.4 mi.

AMERICAN AVE.

Oracle Jct.

5.5 mi.

TO BIOSPHERE
2 mi.

"Mt. Lemmon"

MT. LEMMON HWY.

3.2 mi.

pavement ends

5 mi.

38

PEPPERSAUCE
CPGR.

parking

100 yds.

38

15 yds.

wash

29

collecting

ORACLE RD.

20.4 mi.

77

TO PHOENIX

10

N

PRINCE RD.

1.9 mi.

Exit 254

TO TUCSON
5 mi.

This is a great place to spend some time. The region offers pleasant scenery, as well as lots of mineral collecting opportunities. All of the main roads are well graded dirt and gravel, and should not present a problem to most vehicles, if driven carefully.

Lots of copper was found here and associated ores, including colorful chrysocolla, malachite and bornite can be found on numerous dumps. In addition, near Washington Camp, specimens filled with glistening pyrite are not uncommon, some in combination with vivid green epidote and quartz.

The dumps at Duquesne boast cubic crystals of pyrite, as well as malachite, calcite and tiny quartz crystals. The Harshaw Mine also provides pyrite and other minerals.

The accompanying map provides only a general overview of the region. The hills are actually filled with old abandoned mines, all of which offer good collecting potential. Much of the mineral crystallization is concealed within the host rock, requiring suspect stones to be split in order to properly ascertain what might be hidden inside. Be sure to wear goggles if you do crack rocks.

In addition, be advised that the ownership status of these mines change from time to time. A dump that was open to collectors yesterday might now be closed, and vice versa. Always ascertain current collecting status before trespassing. Do not enter any shafts, since some are very unstable, and could collapse at the slightest provocation.

PATAGONIA MINING AREA

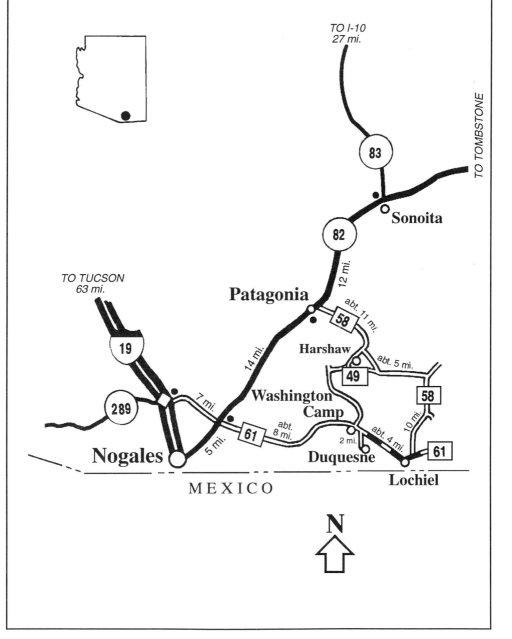